La 5/7 Fighters

in action

By Hans-Heiri Stapfer

Color by Don Greer

Illustrated by Ernesto Cumpian and Richard Hudson

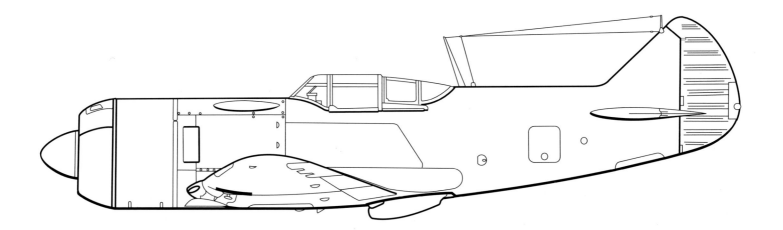

Aircraft Number 169

squadron/signal publications

The Allies top ace, Ivan N. Kozhedub, claims a Messerschmitt Bf 109G during OPERATION CITADEL, the German counter-offensive at Kursk during the summer of 1943. Kozhedub ended the war with 62 aerial victories, claiming them all in La-5s and La-7s. The inscription on his La-5FN reads: 'From the Kolkhoze - Workers of Konyev'.

Acknowledgements

Ladislav Valousek	Frantisek Fajtl
Zdenek Hurt	Dusan Mikolas
Zdenek Titz	Stan Dudek
Bohumir Kudlicka	Kbely Air Force Museum
Ivan Ivanov	Robert Bock
Andrzej Morgala	Carl-Fredrik Geust
Wolfgang Tamme	George Punka
Lennart Andersson	Nigel A. Eastaway
R.A.R.T.	Heinz J. Nowarra
Karl Hänggi	Yefim Gordon
William Rellstab	388th BG Association
Stephan Boshniakov	Harry Wisch
S.H.A.A.	

Dedication:

This book is dedicated to two Czechoslovak Lavochkin pilots:
Ladislav Valousek and Frantisek Fajtl.
Without their generous help, a considerable part of this "In Action" would never have been written.

ISBN 0-89747-392-2

If you have any photographs of aircraft, armor, soldiers or ships of any nation, particularly wartime snapshots, why not share them with us and help make Squadron/Signal's books all the more interesting and complete in the future. Any photograph sent to us will be copied and the original returned. The donor will be fully credited for any photos used. Please send them to:

Squadron/Signal Publications, Inc.
1115 Crowley Drive
Carrollton, TX 75011-5010

Если у вас есть фотографии самолётов, вооружения, солдат или кораблей любой страны, особенно, снимки времён войны, поделитесь с нами и помогите сделать новые книги издательства Эскадрон/Сигнал ещё интереснее. Мы переснимем ваши фотографии и вернём оригиналы. Имена приславших снимки будут сопровождать все опубликованные фотографии. Пожалуйста, присылайте фотографии по адресу:

Squadron/Signal Publications, Inc.
1115 Crowley Drive
Carrollton, TX 75011-5010

軍用機、装甲車両、兵士、軍艦などの写真を所持しておられる方はいらっしゃいませんか？どの国のものでも結構です。作戦中に撮影されたものが特に良いのです。Squadron/Signal社の出版する刊行物において、このような写真は内容を一層充実し、興味深くすることができます。当方にお送り頂いた写真は、複写の後お返しいたします。出版物中に写真を使用した場合は、必ず提供者のお名前を明記させて頂きます。お写真は下記にご送付ください。

Squadron/Signal Publications, Inc.
1115 Crowley Drive
Carrollton, TX 75011-5010

(Right) The Lavochkin La-5FN was an outstanding fighter design and became the first Soviet fighter with performance superior to that of the German Messerschmitt Bf 109G. These La-5FNs were assigned to the 1st Czechoslovak Fighter Regiment. Czechoslovakia was the sole operator of the La-5 outside the Soviet Union. The La-5 series was the most widely used radial engined fighter in the Soviet Air Force with 9,920 built during World War Two or, as it is known in Russia, 'The Great Patriotic War'. (Ladislav Valousek)

Introduction

The wooden, radial engined La-5 fighters from the drawing board of the Lavochkin Design Bureau played a vital role in wresting air superiority from the Luftwaffe on the Eastern front. The top scoring Allied ace, Ivan N. Kozhedub, claimed all of his 62 aerial victories while flying Lavochkin fighters. Kozhedub flew his initial combat sorties during OPERATION CITADEL north of Kursk, where he downed four enemy aircraft and claimed his last victim, an Me 262 jet fighter, on 15 February 1945. A considerable number of Soviet aces claimed their kills in Lavochkin fighters. Along with the inline engined Yakovlev fighters, the Lavochkins were the backbone of the Soviet Fighter Aviation Regiments during the Great Patriotic War. Soviet factories built 9,920 La-5s up to November of 1944 when production switched to the more advanced La-7. The same factories built 5,905 La-7s until production ceased in December of 1945.

During the closing years of the 1930s, fighters being produced in the Soviet Union were unique in one respect — no other country was mass producing modern fighters made of wood. Reports from various Soviet research institutes had established that metal, given the same strength requirements, was forty percent lighter than wood. Additionally, the advantages of metal's durability, fire resistance, and ability to withstand severe climatic conditions were well known to Soviet scientists. Nevertheless, the light metal alloys used in Western aircraft construction were in desperately short supply in the USSR, whereas wood was available in nearly unlimited quantities. Additionally, wood did not require the same level of highly skilled labor needed to form and assemble metal alloys. Therefore, it is not surprising that the prototypes of the three modern fighters (LaGG-3, MiG-3 and Yak-1) were all built of wood.

The first weeks of war with Nazi Germany had proved the concept of building great quantities of fighters using wood rather than the more sophisticated light metal alloys. After the first few months of the campaign, Soviet production of light alloys had dropped by eighty percent, leaving wood as the primary material in new fighter construction.

La-5 Prototype

The experiences of Soviet pilots with the in-line engined LaGG-3 during the early days of the Great Patriotic War were disastrous. The aircraft was openly referred to as a 'mortician's mate' — an aircraft whose intentions towards its pilots were no more benevolent than the aircraft and pilots of the Luftwaffe. This censure of the LaGG-3 was not without justification since the fighter revealed much evidence of the haste with which it had been tested and committed to production. All but the most experienced pilots found it a difficult machine to fly. It was overweight, under powered, and unforgiving. While the LaGG-3 was regarded as obsolete in early 1942 by the Commissariat of the People for the Aviation Industry (NKAP), production continued until the moment preparations were made to convert the production lines to more advanced fighters.

Shortly after the German invasion in June of 1941 an order was issued to the Design Bureaus of Lavochkin, Mikoyan-Gurevich (MiG), and Yakovlev to adapt the M-82 radial engine to their fighter airframes as a possible alternative to the inline engine. The Kremlin regarded the development of experimental radial-engined versions of the LaGG-3, MiG-3, and Yak-7 as a safeguard in the event output of the in-line Klimov and Mikulin engines suffered during the move of Soviet factories to new complexes far behind the Ural mountains.

The 1676 horsepower (hp) M-82 radial engine had been developed by Arcadiy D. Shvetsov and his team in their Design Bureau at Perm in central Russia. Shortly after the end of State Acceptance Trials, large scale production of the M-82 powerplant began in May of 1941. Any interruption in production was unlikely since the factory was in Perm, far beyond the range of Luftwaffe bombers. Although the radial engined prototypes from the MiG and Yakovlev Design Bureaus remained unique, the Lavochkin proposal became one of the most successful fighters of World War II.

Semyon Mikhailovich Alexeyev, the deputy of Semyon Alekseevich Lavochkin at State Aircraft Factory 21 at Nizhny-Novgorod, was in charge of the radial engine conversion program. He would also be responsible for designing the La-5's successor — the La-7. (After the war Alexeyev established his own Design Bureau and built the Rolls Royce Derwent powered I-215 jet fighter that flew for the first time in December 1947.) Alexeyev's conversion work began in late September of 1941 immediately after the main design bureau had been evacuated from the Moscow suburb of Khimki to Nizhny-Novgorod during the fall of 1941. The new radial engined fighter was designated the La-5.

A standard LaGG-3 was taken from the production line to serve as the prototype aircraft equipped with the M-82 radial engine. Grafting the 1260mm (49.6 inches) diameter M-82 radial engine to a LaGG-3 fuselage designed to mount a 777mm (30.5 inches) wide Klimov M-105 in-line powerplant was no easy task. The design was further complicated by the differing thrust lines of the engines and substantially greater weight (by 250kg/551 lbs) of the radial engine. However, the 1676 hp M-82 radial engine, originally developed for the Su-2 bomber, offered considerably more power than the 1100 hp Klimov M-105PA engine used in the LaGG-3.

The M-82 aero engine ultimately became the most successful Soviet radial engine of World War II with a total of some 71,000 powerplants built in 22 different variants. The M-82 powered both the La-5 and the Tu-2 bomber. The M-82 was also installed in various prototypes of the MiG, Petlyakov, Polikarpov, Sukhoi and Yakovlev Design Bureaus. A special derivative, called ASh-82V was used after World War II on the Mil Mi-4 and the Yakovlev Yak-24 helicopters.

A close fitting, tapered cowling was adopted and equipped with adjustable front louvers to control the flow of cooling air around the engine. Front and rear fans were also adopted for warm weather operations. The carburetor intakes mounted in the leading edge of the wing roots of the LaGG-3 were eliminated.

Semyon Alekseevich Lavochkin, one of the most outstanding aircraft designers of the Soviet Union, stands in front of his La-5F fighters during 1943. After the war Lavochkin was responsible for designing a number of missiles, including the SA-2 'Guideline' surface-to-air missile used during the Vietnam War. (Ivan Ivanov)

Since the La-5 prototype was converted from a standard production LaGG-3, the cockpit and rear fuselage were nearly identical to the piston engined Lavochkin fighter. Fuel capacity and much of the internal equipment was also unchanged. The prototype La-5 did, however, lack the leading-edge automatic slats and retractable tail wheel of the late production LaGG-3. Both items were later reintroduced on the La-5 production line.

A further modification on the prototype was the elimination of the ventral engine coolant radiator and its fairing — both rendered unnecessary by the air-cooled radial engine. As a result the aerodynamics around the lower aft fuselage were greatly improved. The oil cooler under the nose remained, but it was repositioned to the rear and cowled under a smaller fairing. The long exhaust pipes of the LaGG-3 were eliminated. The exhaust manifolds of the radial engine were clustered together into a single outlet on each side of the forward fuselage to afford some measure of thrust augmentation. The pipes were covered with a rectangular metal plate.

The M-82 engine turned a new VISh-105V propeller, while contemporary LaGG-3s were still equipped with the VISh-61P propeller. This modification resulted in a slightly enlarged spinner when compared with the LaGG-3. The enlarged spinner was necessary to cover a pair of balance weights used by the VISh-105V propeller's R-7 reduction gearing. The hub and spinner incorporated a Hucks-type starter dog for starting the engine when compressed air was not available for the self-starter.

Compared with the contemporary LaGG-3 (29th Series), the overall length of the La-5 prototype was slightly reduced from 8.81 meters (28.9 feet) to 8.67 meters (28.4 feet). Due to the heavier engine, the take-off weight was raised from the LaGG-3's 3160kgs (6966 lbs) to 3380kgs (7451 lbs) on the La-5 prototype.

Combat experience on the Eastern Front clearly demonstrated the superiority of large caliber weapons over fast firing, rifle caliber machine guns. This had an influence on the La-5 prototype. The general armament of the earlier LaGG-3s consisted of a 20mm ShVAK cannon and a Berezin UBS 12.7mm machine gun. The La-5 prototype was armed with two belt-fed, gas operated 20mm ShVAK cannons mounted in the upper forward fuselage. Two small blisters were added to the upper fuselage between the engine and the cockpit to clear the guns' breeches.

The La-5 prototype was completed in December of 1941, but ground tests revealed several problems with the new engine configuration which delayed its maiden flight. It was not until March of 1942 that the prototype took to the air for its first flight with Aleksei Ivanovich Nikashin, a highly experienced pilot assigned to the Soviet Air Force Scientific Research Institute, at the controls.[1]

Factory testing of the La-5 revealed that the poor flight characteristics of the LaGG-3 had not been completely overcome on the La-5 prototype. Several detail improvements were made before the La-5 prototype was transferred to the Scientific Research Institute for State Acceptance Trials in early April of 1942.

Although the radial engined prototype was considerably heavier than the LaGG-3, the M-82 engine's greater power offered much improved performance over the LaGG-3. The La-5's speed at sea level was greater by eight kmh (4.9 mph), while the La-5's speed of 600kmh (372 mph) at 6450 meters (21,161 feet) was 34kmh (21 mph) higher than that of the LaGG-3 at 6000 meters (19,685 feet). The climb rate was also superior with the La-5 requiring only six minutes to reach 5000 meters (16,404 feet). The results were promising in one other aspect — a captured German Bf 109F-2 was found to be slightly inferior to the La-5 prototype, whereas the LaGG-3 had been completely outclassed by the Messerschmitt.

Overall, the evaluation by the Scientific Research Institute demonstrated the superiority of the radial engined Lavochkin over the inline engined LaGG-3 and that it had the potential for being an excellent fighter — at least by Soviet Air Force standards of the time. Trials lasted less than a month and the aircraft was cleared for mass production by the NKAP. Production began in July of 1942.

Since it was not totally clear at the time if the M-82 radial engine project would be successful, development of the inline powered LaGG-3 at the Lavochkin design bureau continued. For a time the LaGG-3 and the La-5 were built alongside each other at State Aircraft Factories and new features and improvements were simultaneously introduced in both types.

1(Nikashin was later killed on 12 June 1943 during the maiden flight of the Gudkov Gu-1 — a fighter that resembled the US-built Bell P-39 Airacobra. This incident also marked the end of Mikhail Ivanovich Gudkov's career in aircraft design...)

The LaGG 3, powered by a 1100 hp Klimov M-105 inline engine, suffered greatly at the hands of the Luftwaffe and was disliked by the pilots who flew it. Additional power seemed to be the answer. (Zdenek Ondra)

The La-5 prototype had 14-cylinder M-82 radial engine installed in a standard production LaGG-3 airframe. It first flew in March of 1942. (Ivan Ivanov)

La-5 Prototype

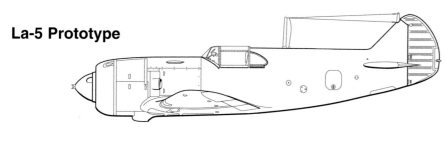

La-5 '206'

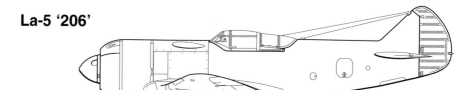

La-5 Standard

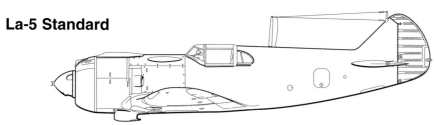

La-7

La-5F

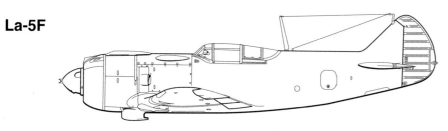

La-7 (Three Cannon)

La-5FN

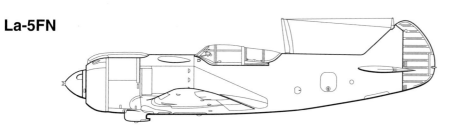

La-7R

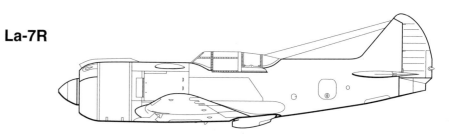

La-5UTI

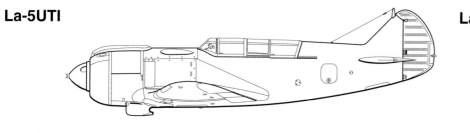

La-7UTI

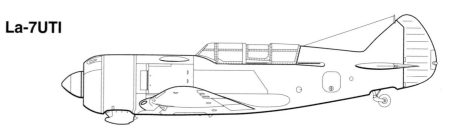

Lavochkin La-5

Flight trials of the La-5 prototype clearly demonstrated that it was superior in all respects to the LaGG-3 and the La-5 was ordered into production. The first aircraft left the assembly lines in July of 1942. Apart from the ASh-82A radial engine, the La-5's airframe was nearly identical to the contemporary LaGG-3 (now the 35th Series) and for a time the two were produced side by side at Nizhny-Novgorod.

Production La-5s differed in a number of minor details from the prototype. First and foremost, the 1676 hp ASh-82 engine used on the La-5 prototype was replaced by the new 1700 hp ASh-82A powerplant. The first production ASh-82A engines left the production lines at the Perm engine factory in April of 1942. The engine oil cooler housing was squared off and enlarged below the cowling. A carburetor air intake was fitted into the upper lip of the cowl. A bulged, centerline fairing was also added to the upper surface of the cowl. The housing for the exhaust stub collector was enlarged and covered with a rectangular exhaust shield. Production La-5s also featured larger bulges over the front fuselage cannon breeches.

The engine's maximum continuous power was 1540 hp at 2050 meters (6725 feet) using a 7 to 1 compression ratio and a two-speed supercharger. The M-82A was equipped with an AK-82BP carburetor, a BSM-14 ignition system, a Type RPD-1M pressure regulator, and a GS-350 generator. Fuel was provided from the five wing tanks via a BNK-10 fuel pump. The M-82A was designed to use 94 octane fuel. The VISh-105V three-blade, controllable-pitch propeller with R-7 reduction gear was retained from the prototype.

The wing of the La-5 was slightly modified when automatic slats were introduced on the wing leading edge. The addition of slats required moving the pitot tube from the starboard wing leading edge to a position under the wing. A trim tab was added to the inner edge of each aileron. The wing fuel tank filler ports were combined into a single port and the single landing light in the port wing leading edge was eliminated.

Behind the engine and engine accessory bay the La-5's structure was virtually identical to that of the earlier LaGG-3 fighter. Its fuselage was a semi-monocoque design with plywood-sheathed birch frames, triangular section wooden stringers, and bakelite ply skinning. The fuselage had four main longerons and 14 stringers attached to 15 vertical box-frame bulkheads.

The DSP-10 delta wood used on the La-5 was developed at the All-Russian Institute of Aviation Materials at Zhukovsky. It was built from five to eight layers of birch strips, glued cross-grain, and impregnated with VIAM-B3 (phenol-formaldehyde resin, borax, and boric acid) and used in conjunction with bakelite ply. The bakelite ply consisted of layers of birch strip bonded with bakelite film at 150 degrees Celsius.

Delta wood was only used in the first production batches of the La-5, because the imported German resin was soon in short supply. As a result, the delta wood components were replaced by conventional pine. Although the wing spar flanges became thicker, there was no great difference in weight due to the lower weight of the pine versus the heavier treated delta wood.

The two-spar wing used NACA 23016 profiles at the root and NACA 23010 profiles at the wing tips. The front spar was straight along the entire wing while the rear spar was broken at the wing panel joint. The wings were skinned with 3mm (.1 inch) plywood. The slotted aluminum ailerons were fabric covered. The all-metal flaps could be deflected 50 degrees for landing and 10 to 15 degrees in combat to improve the fighter's turning radius.

The five wing fuel tanks held a total volume of 341kg (751 lbs) of fuel. The tanks were made from an aluminum and magnesium alloy overlaid with four layers of phenol-formaldehyde resin-impregnated fabric to a thickness of 8mm (.31 inches). In the event of bullet damage, the resin fabric acted as a self-sealing agent within 10-15 seconds of coming into contact with the fuel. The fuel tanks were automatically filled with cooled, inert exhaust gases to inhibit the risk of fire. Gases from the port exhaust manifold were collected in a tube that led to a filter placed in the rear fuselage. The cleaned and cooled gases were then routed via a pipe to the five fuel tanks. The LaGG-3 and La-5 were the only modern Soviet fighters using exhaust gases to suppress fires in fuel tanks.

The landing gear legs were fitted to the front spar wall and were hydraulically retracted into the wing and fuselage. During operations from muddy airfields it was common to remove the lower main gear door from the main gear strut leaving only the upper strut fairing in place. The main wheels were 650mm (25.5 inches) in diameter and 200mm (7.8 inches) wide. Production La-5s were equipped with a retractable tail wheel covered by a pair of doors. The tail wheel was 300mm (11.8 inches) in diameter by 125mm (4.9 inches) wide and was hydraulically operated. The doors were bulged to provide additional clearance for the wheel. This change was short-lived as the bulged doors were eliminated in favor of flush fitting doors.

The first La-5 production batches were equipped with the pitot tube of the contemporary LaGG-3 versions, but most production La-5s received an enlarged pitot tube.

The La-5's armament consisted of a pair of ShVAK (*Shpitalny-Vladimirova Aviatsionnaya Krupnokalibernaya* [Shpitalny-Vladimirov Large Caliber Cannon]) 20mm cannons mounted in the forward fuselage. The ShVAK had been developed from the highly successful 7.62mm ShKAS machine gun by Boris G. Shpitalny and S. V. Vladimirov. The 20m cannon became available in 1936. It weighed 42kg (92.5 lbs) and fired 750 to 800 rounds per minute. Its overall length was 1760mm (69.2 inches). The barrel alone had a length of 1245mm (49 inches). Each weapon was provided with 200 rounds.

The La-5 prototype and the initial production batches used the windscreen and canopy from the LaGG-3, but later production La-5s were equipped with modified units. The rounded frame

La-5 Prototype

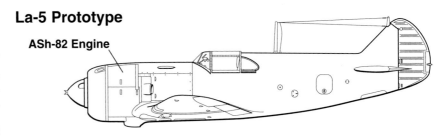

ASh-82 Engine

La-5 Standard

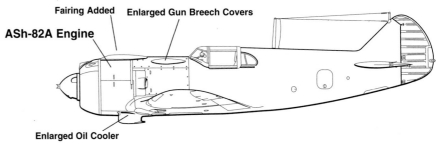

Fairing Added   Enlarged Gun Breech Covers

ASh-82A Engine

Enlarged Oil Cooler

This early production La-5 has a supercharger air intake and trunking similar to the later La-5FN. The aircraft is equipped with an aft sliding canopy similar to that of the LaGG-3 (66th Series), but has the windscreen of the early LaGG-3 versions. (Ivan Ivanov)

Wing Modifications

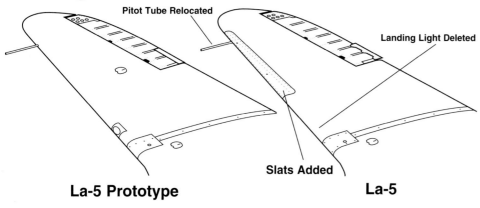

Pitot Tube Relocated

Landing Light Deleted

Slats Added

La-5 Prototype

La-5

The early production La-5 featured an additional door above the main strut cover. This door was deleted on production La-5s. The aerial stub on the tail is also missing and both antenna cables lead directly into the vertical fin's leading edge. (Ivan Ivanov)

of the windscreen was replaced with a rectangular frame and two additional cross frames in order to accommodate a 55mm (2.1 inch) armor glass plate behind the windscreen. The rearmost vertical frame of the aft sliding canopy was also enlarged.

The La-5 was equipped with the PBP-1A (*Prizel dlya Bombometaniya S Pikirovaniya* [Bomb Sight for Dive Bombing]) gun sight. The PBP-1A was a rudimentary lens-type reflector sight with two deflection rings — one for 200 kmh (124 mph) and one for 300 kmh (186 mph). The sight was unable to provide a fine degree of deflection and usually required bursts before, through, and after the target to ensure hits.

All La-5s were equipped to carry D3-40 bomb racks under the wings, however the racks were fitted to only a few aircraft. Bombs up to 50kg (110 lbs) could be carried. Bomb types included the FAB-50 (FAB= *Fugasnaja Avia Bomba* [general purpose bomb]) as well the AO-25M and the FAB-50M fragmentation bombs. The bombs were generally painted gray. Color codes were painted on the bombs to identify their purpose, although these were not always applied. Anti-armor bombs had yellow-red stripes, while fragmentation bombs had green and blue stripes around the body. Practice bombs were painted in white and red.

The cockpit was spartan by German, British, or American standards. Instruments included a KI-10 compass, US-800 speed indicator, VA-30 rate of climb indicator, TE-22 engine revolution counter, TZT-5 engine and oil temperature control instrument, and a Type AVR clock. There were no gyroscopic instruments such as an artificial horizon or gyro compass.

The La-5 could be equipped with an RSI-4 'Malyutka' (RSI=*Radiostancija dlja Istrebitelei* [Radio for Fighter]) radio system, although the system was not carried by all aircraft. The RSI-4 consisted of a transmitter and receiver and usually only the lead aircraft in a formation was equipped with both. The remaining aircraft had either a receiver only or nothing at all. The RSI-4 'Malyutka' operated with variable frequencies in a band between 3.7 and 6.05 Megacycles. Frequency selection was by means of a knob under the starboard side of the instrument panel. Both the receiver and transmitter were powered by an RU-11A accumulator. The system weighed 2kg (4.4 lbs).

The initial production batches were equipped with 10mm (.39 inch) armor plate behind the pilot's seat. Later production batches were provided with 8.5mm (.33 inch) armor plate in order to save weight.

By Western standards, the La-5 was an austere and unsophisticated aircraft. Nevertheless, its sturdy wooden structure, lack of complexity, and its limited demands on field maintenance made it perfectly suitable for the role and conditions in which it was operated by the Soviet Air Force — conditions which would have resulted in a much lower rate of serviceability with a more sophisticated fighter.

Despite the design's promise, however, the first production La-5s had a remarkably lower performance than the prototype, suffering a 40 to 50 kmh (24.8 to 31 mph) loss in top speed. Investigations by the Central Aero Hydrodynamics Institute (TsAGI) at Zhukovsky indicated that the primary reason for the performance loss was drag from the handmade, ill-fitting engine cowling and the poor sealing of the engine accessory bay panels.

Another problem area was the poor view from the cockpit that was worsened by the greater bulk of the radial engine. A high vibration rate at cruising speeds, caused by the poor mounting of the engine to the fuselage, was also a problem. Operational evaluations of the La-5 also showed that it was impossible to use the PBP-1A sight properly when the two ShVAK cannons were fired due to excessive vibration. To make things worse, two La-5s crashed after losing a wing. One of the fighters was in a landing approach, while the other was in a shallow dive. A crash program was instituted in order to solve the problems while the La-5 remained in production. The pilot's seat was raised to provide a better field of view in all directions, the wing mounts were reinforced, cannon installations were revised, and vibrations were eliminated by improving the balance of the propeller.

During October of 1942 the Scientific Research Institute at Sverdlovsk tested a production La-5. Compared to the prototype, the production La-5 suffered a slight loss of speed at sea level (down to 509 kmh/316 mph) and a loss of 20 kmh (12.4 mph) in top speed. The lower speeds came despite the production aircraft weighing 20kg (44 lbs) less at 3360kg (7407 lbs) and needing only 22.6 seconds to complete a 360 degree turn versus the prototype's 25 seconds.

By October of 1942, however, the standard German fighter on the Eastern Front was the Messerschmitt Bf 109G-2 equipped with the Daimler-Benz DB 605A engine. A Messerschmitt Bf 109 G-2/R6 (Serial Number 13903), captured in the Stalingrad area, was test flown against an La-5. The German fighter proved to be superior to the La-5 in most respects. The Bf 109G-2 had a top speed of 623 kmh (387 mph) and a service ceiling of 11,750 meters (38,549 feet) — 1750 meters (5741 feet) higher than the La-5. The La-5 was slightly faster than the Bf 109G-2 at sea level and could out turn the German fighter. While the La-5 was armed with two ShVAK 20m cannons, the Messerschmitt's armament consisted of one 20mm MG-151 cannon and two 13mm MG-131 heavy machine guns.

The first La-5s were assigned to Fighter Aviation Regiments during the fall of 1942. Pilots with previous experience in the I-16, MiG-3, and LaGG-3 were quickly accustomed to their new mounts and were pleased with its improved performance. The ground crews also welcomed the new aircraft since the lack of a liquid cooling system made the La-5 easier to maintain in the field and helped enhance the La-5's service rate.

La-5s saw combat on every major front from the fall of 1942 to the summer of 1943 before they started to be replaced by more advanced versions of the fighter. Some La-5s remained in front line service well into 1944. During the fall of 1942 the first La-5s were deployed directly from the production lines to the Stalingrad sector. The La-5 also fought the Luftwaffe's Luftflotte 4 in the battle over the Kuban river in the North Caucasus during April and May of 1943.

The La-5 saw considerable action during the battle of Kursk in July of 1943 when the

Canopy Development

La-5 Early

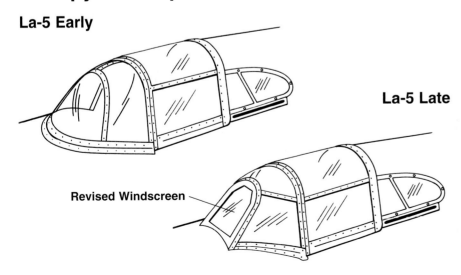

Revised Windscreen

La-5 Late

Pilots of the 159th Fighter Aviation Regiment prepare for a mission on the Kuban Front in May of 1943. The inscription on the fuselage of the La-5 (white 60) reads 'Valerij Chkalov Squadron'. The unit carried the name in honor of a famous and very popular Soviet test pilot who was killed on 15 December 1938 while testing the Polikarpov I-180 fighter. (Ivan Ivanov)

An La-5 taxies out for a mission on a field near Belgorod during the Battle of Kursk in the summer of 1943. La-5s assigned to this sector took part in actions against Luftwaffe aircraft of Luftflotte 4 (4th Air Fleet). The La-5 has a natural metal exhaust panel, a white spinner, and a yellow rudder. (Ivan Ivanov)

A pair of La-5s run up their engines prior to a mission near Belgorod during OPERATION CITADEL — the German offensive against the Red Army during the summer of 1943. Both aircraft, white 65 in foreground and white 24 in the background, have the vertical fin tip painted yellow. (Ivan Ivanov)

La-5s line up on another hastily built airstrip near Belgorod during the summer of 1943. The La-5 nearest the camera has a yellow-black spinner, while the second fighter has an all black spinner. The first La-5 has an ASh-82F engine logo painted on the cowling. (Ivan Ivanov)

Wehrmacht deployed approximately 2,700 tanks and self propelled guns for OPERATION CITADEL. By the end of the battle in August of 1943, the Wehrmacht had lost 500,000 troops, 1500 tanks, and over 3,700 aircraft. During the intense air action over Kursk on 6 July 1943, Ivan N. Kozhedub, later to be the Soviet Union's top ace, made his combat debut in an La-5. Coming from a Ukrainian peasant background, Ivan Kozhedub, at the age of twenty-three, had the requisite humble origins to become an important Soviet war hero. As with many great aces, Kozhedub's first encounter with the enemy nearly proved fatal. Flying a combat sortie north of Kursk, Kozhedub lost contact with his leader. Alone, he sighted a formation of German aircraft and recklessly dived toward them. His attack, if unexpected, did little damage and he was soon being aggressively pursued by a pair of Messerschmitt Bf-109s which were firing accurately and at close range. Kozhedub abruptly brought his damaged La-5 to lower altitudes to elude his pursuers and then flew at tree-top level back to the Soviet lines. The damaged La-5, easily mistaken for the Focke Wulf Fw 190, drew sporadic fire from Soviet anti-aircraft batteries which shot away one of its wing tips. Kozhedub was eventually able to make a safe landing. Having learned a valuable lesson about trying to fight the war by himself, Ivan N. Kozhedub was back in action and by the third day of OPERATION CITADEL had destroyed two Junkers Ju 87 dive bombers and two Messerschmitt Bf 109 fighters. Ivan N. Kozhedub was awarded the Order of the Red Banner at the end of the Battle of Kursk.

The La-5 camouflage scheme of black and green upper surfaces over light blue under surfaces was carried over from the earlier LaGG-3 fighters. Soviet national markings were applied on the fuselage sides, vertical fin, and the lower wing surfaces. They were not applied to the upper wing surfaces. The red underwing star was small with a black outline. Most of the factories delivered La-5s with a large, black outlined red star on the fuselage and tail. During the fall of 1943, the La-5s that remained in operational service received the new style of national marking — a red star with a large white outline and a thin red border. A tactical number was usually applied to the rear fuselage. A number of La-5s had the rudder painted yellow.

During the winter of 1942 and 1943, a number of La-5s were given a coat of coarse white paint over the upper surfaces. Only the national markings on the fuselage and the tactical number were not covered by the thick layers of paint. The temporary winter camouflage resulted in a poor surface finish and reduced the top speed by some 10 kmh (6.2 mph).

The Germans were also interested in the new Soviet fighter and one of the first La-5 captured intact by the Germans was flown by Lieutenant Colonel Nikolai Vlasov. On 30 July 1943 Vlasov was on inspection of flying personnel of the 275th Fighter Division when he made an emergency landing with La-5 (white 6) at Larisov near Ostrov. A second intact La-5 (white 84) assigned to the Valerij Chkalov Squadron of the 159th Fighter Aviation Regiment was tested at the Luftwaffe's Test and Evaluation Center at Rechlin. The captured La-5 had been camouflaged in black-green and dark green on the upper surfaces and light blue on the under surfaces. The spinner was painted in either light blue, silver, or black-green. The propeller was painted in black-green.

During 1942 a total of 1,129 La-5 fighters were produced. The State Aircraft Factory 21 at Nizhny-Novgorod built 1,107 aircraft while the State Aircraft Factory 31 at Tbilisi built a further 22 of the radial engine fighter. In contrast, a total of 2,771 LaGG-3s were built during the same year. The La-5s were regarded as an interim variant in order to quickly adopt M-82/ASh-82A radial engines without causing a major disruption of the production lines. This gave the Lavochkin Design Bureau time to develop a more sophisticated version of the fighter and eliminating the La-5s shortcomings such as insufficient range and rear vision. The last Shvetsov M-82F powered La-5s were delivered during early 1943.

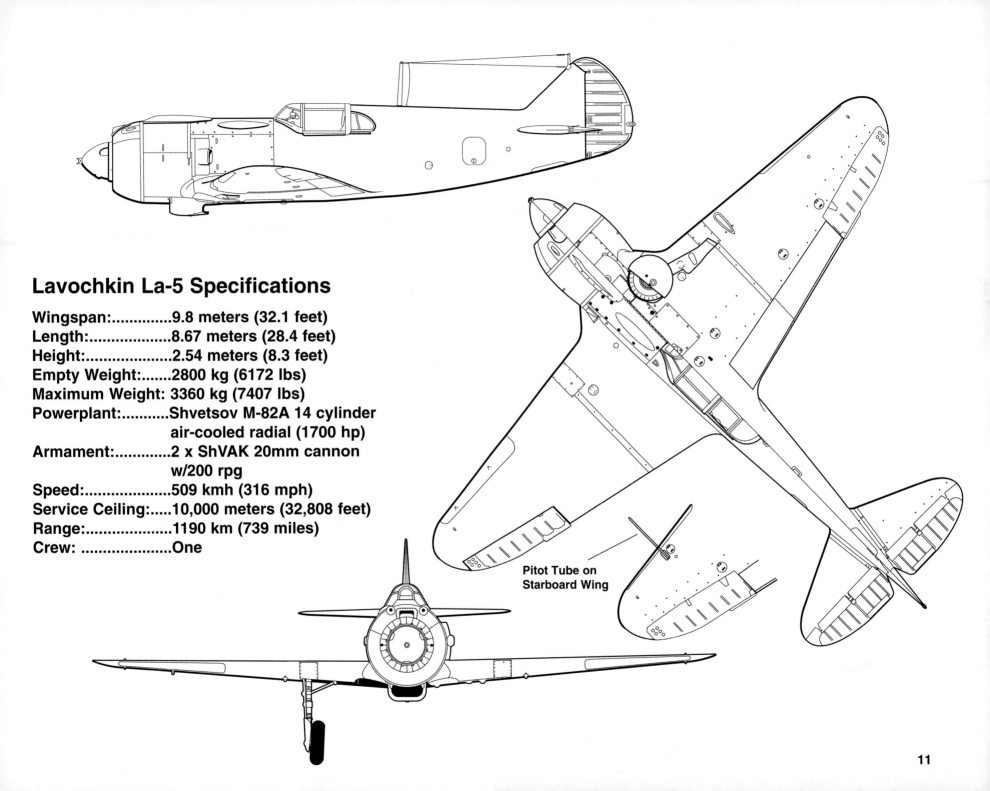

Lavochkin La-5 Specifications

Wingspan:..............9.8 meters (32.1 feet)
Length:..................8.67 meters (28.4 feet)
Height:..................2.54 meters (8.3 feet)
Empty Weight:.......2800 kg (6172 lbs)
Maximum Weight: 3360 kg (7407 lbs)
Powerplant:...........Shvetsov M-82A 14 cylinder
                            air-cooled radial (1700 hp)
Armament:.............2 x ShVAK 20mm cannon
                            w/200 rpg
Speed:...................509 kmh (316 mph)
Service Ceiling:.....10,000 meters (32,808 feet)
Range:...................1190 km (739 miles)
Crew: ....One

Pitot Tube on
Starboard Wing

Lavochkin La-5F

The La-5F derived its name from the new ASh-82F (F for *Forsirovanny* [Boosted]) engine. When Arcadiy D. Shvetsov placed the original ASh-82A powerplant into production at GAZ-19 in Perm during May of 1942, it was to produce as many engines as possible. As a result the ASh-82A was considered 'immature' when it made its service debut in the La-5. Cylinder head temperatures were critical and had to be kept between 200 and 220 degrees Celsius. There were numerous instances of the cylinders literally losing their heads when the pilot failed to keep an eye on the cylinder head temperature gauge. The loss of the cylinder heads and, in some cases, the complete disintegration of the cylinders posed a serious problem for the Shvetsov Design Bureau during the ASh-82A early service. Attempts to alleviate the problem and increase the engine's power resulted in the ASh-82F.

The ASh-82F had the same output as the earlier ASh-82A, but provided improved performance at altitudes above 1500 meters (4921 feet). At 1650 meters (5413 feet) the ASh-82F was rated at 1676 hp, while at 4650 meters (15,255 feet) the engine was still putting out 1450 hp. Like the ASh-82A, the ASh-82F was operated with a conventional carburetor. Externally the introduction of the new engine did not bring about any changes to the cowling apart from the application of the 'Forsirovanny' logo (a red Cyrillic 'F' in a yellow circle) on both sides of the engine cowling. The logos were sometimes not applied and were sometimes overpainted in the field.

The first ASh-82F powerplants were fitted into the last La-5 production batches during December of 1942. The first La-5F left the production lines at the State Aircraft Factory 21 at Nizhny-Novgorod in March of 1943.

Apart from the new engine, the primary differences between the earlier La-5 and the new La-5F was an entirely new canopy that provided the pilot with a much improved view towards the rear. The rear fuselage decking was cut down and a new fixed canopy section was added.

The new canopy provided 360 degrees of vision and incorporated a 66mm (2.5 inch) thick armor glass panel to protect the pilot's head and shoulders. The sliding canopy's rearmost vertical frame was reduced in width.

The windscreen was also redesigned with the La-5F now having a horizontal frame on top of the windscreen. This modification was first made on the La-5 in order to improve the mounting of a 55mm (2.1 inch) thick piece of armor glass behind the windscreen. A rear view mirror was also added to the windscreen, although it was sometimes removed by the pilots in the field.

The PBP-1A (Prizel dlya Bombometaniya S Pikirovaniya [Bomb Sight for Dive Bombing]) of the La-5 was replaced by the more advanced PBP-1B gun sight which had a lens-type reflector of about two inches in diameter. There were two deflection rings, one for 200 kmh (124 mph) and the other for 300 kmh (186 mph). Like the earlier PBP-1A, however, no fine degree of deflection could be obtained.

A small inlet was placed on each side of the fuselage just below the windscreen to improve the cockpit ventilation. Poor insulation of the engine bay and inadequate ventilation had resulted in high cockpit temperatures in the La-5.

Initial La-5F production aircraft had the same radio mast and antenna configuration as the La-5. Most of the La-5Fs, however, were built with a thicker, forward slanting mast. On the La-5 and the first production La-5Fs, both wire antennas ran from the mast to the root and tip of the aerial stub on the tail. On La-5Fs with the forward slanted mast, only a single wire ran between the mast and the aerial stub on the tail fin. A second wire ran from the aerial stub to a small blister fitted on the port side of the fuselage next to the aerial mast.

The La-5F retained the fuel tank construction and the inert exhaust gas fire suppression system of the La-5, however, the two 65 liter (17 US gal) fuel tanks in the outer wing panels were deleted. Their use had been largely restricted to ferry flights and their removal, together with

This early La-5F is missing part of the upper engine cowl and is equipped with the early vertical antenna mast. The aircraft carries the later style of national markings introduced in early 1944 and has had the tail painted white. (Yefim Gordon)

La-5/La-5F Development

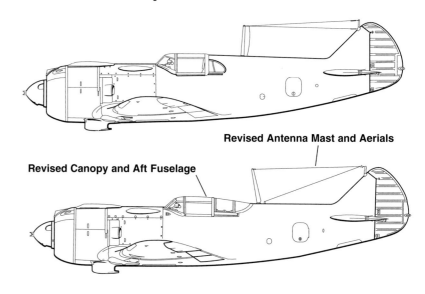

Revised Antenna Mast and Aerials

Revised Canopy and Aft Fuselage

other airframe refinements, resulted in a weight savings of 160kg (352 lbs). Due to the reduced fuel capacity the La-5F's range dropped to 760 km (472 miles) versus the 1190 km (739 miles) range of the La-5. The primary purpose of the weight saving efforts was to match the performance of the current versions of the Messerschmitt Bf 109G.

During the production of the La-5F, the delta wood portion in the structure was gradually reduced and the components were replaced by conventional pine. The wing spar flanges became thicker, but there was little weight penalty since the pine weighed less.

The wings of most La-5Fs had the main spars made of fir while the wing ribs were made of fir strips and plywood. The wing skins were made from of 3mm (.1 inch) birch plywood. Late production La-5Fs had the wooden spars replaced by metal spars made from steel angle beams joined by duralumin walls. La-5Fs equipped with the all-metal spars had the original three tank configuration of the wooden-spar version replaced by four tanks — all located between the main spars. The two center tanks held 168 liters (44.3 US gal) of fuel each while the outer tanks each contained 148 liters (39 US gal). There was no external difference between the wood and metal sparred wings.

The small blister on the main gear door was also redesigned. The round blister on the La-5 landing gear door gave way to a rectangular blister on the La-5F.

During April of 1943 one of the new La-5F fighters was tested at the Soviet Air Force's Scientific Research Institute at Sverdlovsk. The La-5F had a speed of 557 kmh (346 mph) at sea level and a top speed of 590 kmh (366.6 mph) at 6200 meters (20,341 feet) — only 10 kmh (6.2 mph) more than the La-5. The climb rate, however, was much improved with the La-5F needing only 5.5 minutes to climb to 5000 meters (16,404 feet) versus the La-5's six minutes.

The La-5F served primarily with the Fighter Aviation Regiments assigned to Air Armies on the Eastern Front, but were also allocated to the Fighter Aviation Regiments of the National Air Defense Forces (PVO). The units of the National Air Defense Forces were assigned to

Landing Gear Doors

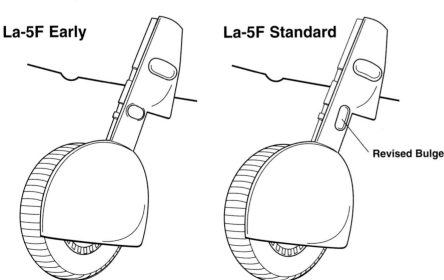

La-5F Early

La-5F Standard

Revised Bulge

The show room of the Central Aero Hydrodynamics Institute (TsAGI) at Zhukovsky displays an early, overall white La-5F during 1943. The La-5F introduced the cut down rear fuselage and rear canopy glazing that would be retained for the remainder of the La-5 and La-7 production. (Ivan Ivanov)

This black and black-green camouflaged La-5F (white 20) was assigned to the 159th Fighter Aviation Regiment. The inscription on the fuselage reads 'Valerij Chkalov Squadron'. Black and black-green camouflaged La-5s were not often seen since the aircraft was introduced when the two-tone grey schemes were in use. (Nigel Eastaway/RART)

Antenna Mast Development

La-5F Early

Vertical Mast

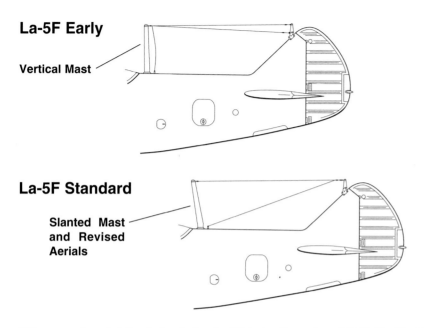

La-5F Standard

Slanted Mast and Revised Aerials

Officers receive a briefing in front of an La-5F during the spring of 1944. Most La-5Fs carried a Forsirovanny (Boosted) logo on both sides of the engine cowling. The logo consisted of a red Cyrillic 'F' on a yellow disc. The engine's front cooling vanes are closed. (Ivan Ivanov)

defend large cities and industrial centers in the USSR against German air attacks. Since the Luftwaffe never carried out a large-scale strategic air campaign against the Soviet Union, the units of the National Air Defense Forces played only a minor role during the Great Patriotic War.

During World War II the USAAF 8th and 15th Air Forces carried out several bombing raids against the Third Reich from Soviet territory. The first shuttle raid took place on 2 June 1944 when 128 Boeing B-17 Flying Fortresses, escorted by 64 North American P-51 Mustangs, took off from their bases in Italy and headed for the railroad marshaling yards at Debrecen, Hungary. After bombing the yards the force headed for the Soviet airfields at Poltava and Mirgorod in the Ukraine. The air cover over the Soviet bases was provided by the 210th Fighter Aviation Division of the National Air Defense Forces. Included in some of the units were Fighter Aviation Regiments equipped with the La-5F, which were based alongside the American bombers at Poltava and Mirgorod air bases.

On 21 June 1944 163 B-17s of the 8th Air Force's 3rd Air Division bombed the synthetic oil plant at Ruhland while enroute to bases in the Ukraine. Shortly after midnight, some eighty Junkers Ju 88s and Heinkel He 111s bombed the airfield at Poltava. Forty-four of the 72 B-17s at Poltava were destroyed on the ground and the remainder were all damaged. No Soviet fighter, including the Lavochkins, appeared to engage the Luftwaffe bombers. The disaster helped fuel the growing tensions between the Americans and Soviets associated with the shuttle operations, although the shuttle raids continued into September of 1944.

The camouflage and markings of the early La-5Fs were generally similar to the La-5 — black-green and olive-green upper surfaces with light blue lower surfaces. However, most of the later La-5Fs were delivered in dark gray and medium gray-green upper surfaces over light blue lower surfaces. The plywood skinning over the fuselage, wings, and tail resulted in a very smooth finish. The seams in the plywood were usually puttied over which left the skin almost

Standard production La-5Fs began reaching the front in late spring of 1943. Most La-5Fs were delivered with a black propeller and a dark green spinner. (Yefim Gordon)

Canopy Development

La-5

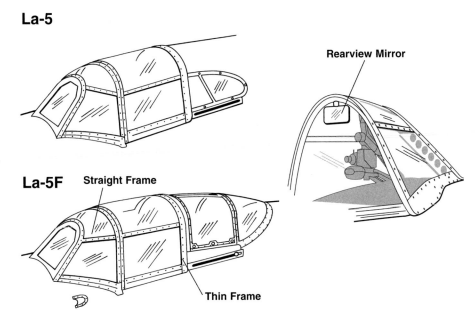

Rearview Mirror

La-5F

Straight Frame

Thin Frame

Ivan N. Kozhedub (right) was the highest scoring Allied ace with 62 kills. He is standing in front of an La-5F assigned to the 240th Fighter Aviation Regiment. The 66mm thick armor glass behind the pilot's head is at the forward end of the aft canopy glazing. A small rearview mirror is hanging from the top of the windscreen. (Robert Bock)

featureless except for the occasional access panel or cover. The metal covered engine and engine accessory bay were another matter. These panels were often dented and scratched due to hurried maintenance in the field. The metal panel immediately behind the exhaust was usually left in a natural metal state. The metal straps holding the cowling together were flexible which resulted in much of the paint flaking off. This could often leave the impression of unpainted silver bands wrapped around the cowl.

The La-5F carried the red star with a small black outline until the fall of 1943 when a new insignia was introduced. The red star was given a wide white outline which was then bordered with a thin red outline. The insignias were applied to the fuselage sides, vertical stabilizer, and the lower wing surfaces. The upper wing surfaces were not marked. A two-digit tactical number was applied to the fuselage side while the fighter was on the production line. The tactical number was the last two digits of the serial number. The numbers were usually applied in white and often had a thin red or black outline and were usually of the same size and style. Some units in the field would repaint the numbers altering the size, shape, or location.

Some La-5Fs received a yellow spinner and a yellow rudder to avoid confusion with the German Focke Wulf Fw 190, which was operated in growing numbers on the Eastern Front. In retrospect, this would seem to be a rather odd system since the German Luftwaffe's Eastern Front theater recognition markings consisted of yellow noses, wing tips, fuselage bands, and rudders.

Captain N. I. Gorbunov of the Grigorij Kovskij Squadron sits in his La-5F at Tiraspol on the North-Western Front during 1944. Captain Gorbunov flew 196 combat missions and destroyed 15 enemy aircraft before he was killed in action on 2 August 1944. The smooth, and somewhat featureless, wooden surfaces of the fuselage and wings contrast sharply with the dented and rippled metal cowl panels. The inlet in front of the windscreen is a typical feature for the La-5F. This particular La-5F also lacks the rear view mirror introduced on most of the La-5Fs. (Ivan Ivanov)

(Above) An La-5F (white 66) of the 21st Fighter Aviation Regiment taxis out for a mission during the summer of 1944. The silver bands on the cowling are flexible metal straps designed to hold the cowl together. Most La-5Fs had a forward slanted antenna mast while the initial production variants had a vertical antenna mast. The cut down rear fuselage and aft canopy glazing of the La-5F greatly improved the pilot's rearward vision over that of the LaGG-3-based La-5. (Ivan Ivanov)

(Below) The La-5F was a subject of great interest to the Germans and was closely examined by the Luftwaffe. The Soviet national markings were painted over and replaced by a Balkenkreuz on the fuselage and a Swastika on the tail. The La-5F was in many respects inferior to the Messerschmitt Bf 109G-6 and the Focke Wulf Fw 190A. Production of the La-5F would eventually give way to the much improved La-5FN. (George Punka)

Guard Lieutenant S. Yasanis (left) and Guard Sub-Lieutenant Kalmytav (right), wearing standard winter flying gear, pose in front of an La-5F during the winter of 1944. (Ivan Ivanov)

Soviet Air Force ground personnel rest in front of an La-5F (white 33). The fighter was part of the 303rd Fighter Aviation Division, 1st Air Army, Tula Airfield during 1944. (SHAA)

Two La-5Fs (white 81 and white 1) and some Yak-9s of the 303rd Fighter Aviation Division are lined up on a field during the battle of Smolensk. White 1's single digit tactical number was unusual. (ECPA)

An La-5F (white 14) of the 21st Fighter Aviation Regiment prepares for take off. The La-5Fs received their large two digit tactical numbers while still on the production line. The numbers were thinly outlined in red. (Ivan Ivanov)

Lavochkin La-5FN

The first La-5FN (FN for *Forsirovanny Neprosredstvenno* [Directly Boosted]) left the State Aircraft Factory 21 in March of 1943 — about the same time the La-5Fs were being delivered to the Fighter Aviation Regiments. The La-5FN is generally considered to be a parallel development of the La-5F rather than its successor.

The La-5FN was powered by an 1850 hp ASh-82FN engine that developed almost 150 more horsepower than the ASh-82F. The ASh-82FN was a further development of the earlier ASh-82F. The power increase, which could be maintained for up to ten minutes, was the result of replacing the carburetors with direct fuel injection. Late production La-5FNs were equipped with the ASh-82FNV powerplant. The engine was still rated at 1850 hp, but offered improved performance at high altitudes. The ASh-82FN engine could be started using compressed air from an internal pressure bottle or using a Hucks-starter dog on the propeller spinner.

The production La-5FN differed from the La-5F in a number of ways. The La-5FN received a long supercharger intake trunk on top of the cowl to support the deeper breathing ASh-82FN engine. The new supercharger intake altered the cowling's support structure and the two retaining buckles on each side of the cowl were deleted. The La-5 and La-5F had the engine exhausts ganged into a single pipe on each side of the fuselage. On the La-5FN, the pipes were split into seven separate outlets in a fashion similar to that of the German BMW 801 engine used on the Fw 190A. The smaller diameter pipes were covered by a single flat plate. Three small louvers were cut into the rear of the exhaust shield to vent the engine accessory and cannon compartments. Late production La-5FNs were equipped with a small circular hatch on the downward hinging engine access doors.

All production La-5FNs were equipped with an additional duralumin fuselage side panel under the cockpit area. These fuselage side panels were not present on the La-5FN prototype.

Early La-5FNs used the radio antenna configuration of the La-5F. The aerial array consisted of a single wire running from the fuselage to the antenna stub on the tail and then to the slanted mast behind the cockpit. Most production La-5FNs, however, reverted to the antenna configuration used on the earlier La-5 with two wires running from the antenna mast to the aerial stub and a small wire lead running from the mast into the fuselage. Late production batches of the La-5FN introduced a further revision to the radio antennas. These aircraft deleted the mast and ran the antenna directly from the vertical fin into the starboard side of the rear canopy glazing. A few aircraft had the wire fitted on the port side of the rear canopy glazing. The first production La-5FNs were equipped with an RSI-4 radio, but this was later changed to the modified RSI-4KhF radio.

Most of the La-5FNs also received thicker armor glass. The first production batches retained the 55mm (2.1 inches) thick armor glass behind the windscreen, but this was changed to 57mm (2.2 inches) on later aircraft. The armor glass behind the pilot was increased from 66mm to 68mm (2.5 to 2.6 inches) as La-5FN production progressed. Some La-5FN returning from repair depots were equipped with an additional vertical frame on the aft-sliding canopy. Later production batches of the La-5FN added a small grab handle to the port side of the outer canopy frame.

In April of 1943 the La-5FN prototype was tested together with a production La-5F at the Scientific Research Institute in Sverdlovsk. The introduction of fuel injection greatly improved the fighter's performance. Top speed at sea level was 595 kmh (369 mph), 38 kmh (23.6 mph) more than the La-5F. Top speed of the La-5FN was 648 kmh (402 mph) at 6300 meters (20,669 feet), a remarkable 58 kmh (36 mph) higher than the La-5F. The climb rate was reduced to 4.7 minutes to reach 5000 meters versus the La-5F's rate of 5.5 minutes to reach the same altitude.

La-5/La-5FN Development

La-5F

La-5FN

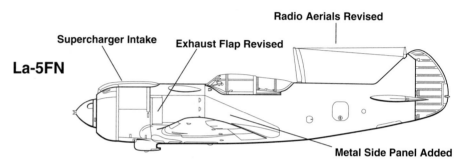

Radio Aerials Revised

Supercharger Intake   Exhaust Flap Revised

Metal Side Panel Added

An early La-5FN (white 95) sits on the ramp during trials at the Scientific Research Institute. The white diamond-shaped 'FN' logo has been painted on the cowl and tail — a common feature of most La-5FNs. (Nigel A. Eastaway)

La-5FN Antenna Mast

La-5FN Early

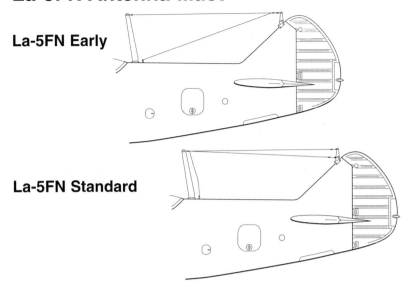

La-5FN Standard

The La-5FN was the first fighter from the Lavochkin Design Bureau to equal the performance of the Messerschmitt Bf 109G-6, which was then the standard Luftwaffe fighter on the Eastern Front. The Bf 109G-6's top speed of 630 kmh (391 mph) was 4 kmh (2.4 mph) less than the La-5FN. However, the La-5FN was still no match for the Focke Wulf Fw-190A-3's top speed of 660 kmh (410 mph).

During April of 1943 a series of mock combat trials were flown at Lyubertsi Air Base between a pre-production La-5FN and a captured Messerschmitt Bf 109G-2. The trials showed that the new La-5FN exceeded the speed of the German fighter at low and medium altitudes where most dog-fights on the Eastern front took place. Additionally, the La-5FN had a distinct advantage over the Messerschmitt when maneuvering in the vertical plane. These trials proved of great value in developing proper combat tactics against the German fighters.

Performance between production batches varied widely and depended greatly on the raw materials and craftsmanship used on each aircraft. Wartime shortages being what they were, such items could vary considerably. In June of 1943 a production La-5FN was pulled off the production line and assigned to the Scientific Research Institute at Sverdlovsk where it underwent a series of comparative tests to the pre-production La-5FNs. At sea level a speed of 583 kmh (362 mph) was recorded, while a top speed of 634 kmh (393 mph) was attained at an altitude of 6250 meters (20,505 feet).

In October of 1944 a captured La-5FN equipped with an ASh-82FNV engine was evaluated by the Luftwaffe at Rechlin. This aircraft had seen extensive service on the Eastern Front before it was captured in September of 1944 at the Gross-Schimanen airfield in East Prussia. At 3347 kg (7378 lbs) the captured La-5FN was 57 kg (125 lbs) heavier than the La-5FN evaluated in June of 1943 at the Soviet Scientific Research Institute. The performance of the captured Lavochkin was remarkably inferior to the new La-5FN tested at Sverdlovsk. At Rechlin the aircraft achieved a speed of 520 kmh (323 mph) at sea level and a top speed of 545 kmh (338 mph) at 6500 meters (21,325 feet). This was almost 89 kmh (55 mph) less than that of the

La-5FN tested in the Soviet Union. The Germans, however, felt that the aircraft displayed good flight characteristics through all phases of flight. Only at high diving speeds — some pilots reached speeds up 720 kmh (447 mph) — did the controls exhibit any stiffness. Additional testing demonstrated that the La-5FN was an excellent low-to-medium altitude fighter and it was particularly suited to a close-in, high-g, maneuvering style of combat. Additionally, the La-5FN had a better rate of climb than its German opponents up to an altitude of 3000 meters (9842 feet).

Shortly after the production of the La-5FN began a weight saving program was initiated in order to improve performance. The Lavochkin Design Bureau decided to replace some wooden parts with light alloy metal parts. Metal wing spars, first introduced toward the end of the La-5F's production run, were standardized on the La-5FN fighter with a weight savings of 172 kg (379 lbs). The first La-5FNs were equipped with three wing tanks, but these were replaced by a series of four tanks in the fighters with metal sparred wings. A fifth, smaller tank was installed behind the engine. The La-5FN continued to use cooled exhaust gases ducted into the fuel tanks as a fire suppression system.

Despite the increase in fuel, the La-5FN's range was reduced due to the engine's greater fuel consumption. Combat mission flight duration was limited to only 40 minutes, but during ferry flights with only 1600 RPM the endurance was 2 hours and 34 minutes.

A reduction of control stick forces was attained by enhanced aerodynamic and static compensation of the control surfaces. These provided a considerable improvement in handling and maneuverability.

La-5FN (white 95) displays the early radio antenna configuration used on the initial production batches. The La-5FN also deleted the single large exhaust stack and introduced multiple stacks covered by a movable flat panel. The '5' of the two digit tactical number is slightly larger than the '9'. (Nigel A. Eastaway)

The fuselage was built in two major subassemblies. The rear section was an assembly of 13 bulkheads and four longerons covered by a skin made of bakelite wood. The thickness of the plywood varied from eight layers (9.5mm/.37 inch) at the cockpit to five (4.5mm/.17 inch) layers at the tail section. The plywood skin was an integral part of the fuselage structure and, with the longerons and bulkheads, formed the semi-monocoque construction.

The front fuselage section included the welded steel tubular engine frame which was connected to fuselage structure by massive wooden beams blended into the fuselage longerons. This structure carried the actual engine mounts, ammunition boxes, fuel and oil tanks. The entire front fuselage section was covered by detachable or hinged metal panels.

The pilot's canopy frame consisted of metal tubing with a sliding center section that could be jettisoned in an emergency. The canopy could be locked in three positions — open, closed, and a mid position for ventilation. The adjustable seat was made of dural sheet and tubes and designed to be used with a seat-pack type parachute. A piece of 10mm (.39 inch) thick armor plate protected the pilot from the rear. On later production batches of the La-5FN, the thickness of the steel armor was reduced to 7mm (.27 inch). The space behind the seat was occupied by an RSI-4KhF radio, battery, oxygen bottle, and the hydraulic and pneumatic systems. The cockpit was not equipped with a heating system.

The landing gear and its hydraulic retraction system were unchanged from the earlier variants, however, the tail wheel retraction system proved to be troublesome and was often disconnected in the field. The aircraft was often flown with the tail wheel locked in the down position.

The La-5FN retained the La-5F's armament of two nose mounted 20 mm ShVAK cannons with 200 rounds per gun. The guns could be charged both pneumatically or mechanically.

Each wing contained provisions for a bomb rack for carrying bombs up to 100kg (220 lbs). The bomb release was placed rather awkwardly very low on the left hand side of the seat. The pilot was forced to bend over to reach it at a point when his full attention should have been devoted to flying the aircraft and hitting the target. Despite the provision for bomb racks, the La-5FN was seldom used for ground support duties. Aside from being vulnerable to ground fire, the bomb release mechanism was unreliable and it was a common occurrence to have one or both bombs hang up on the rack.

La-5FNs were delivered in the now standard scheme of dark grey and medium grey-green. For the most part, the camouflage, national insignia, and tactical markings were identical to those on the La-5F. A few La-5FNs were delivered with a three digit tactical number, but this was rare. Additionally, some aircraft were known to have one of the two digits in the tactical number painted out. Most La-5FN fighters had a white Forsirovanny Neprosredstvenno (Directly Boosted) logo on both sides of the engine cowling and tail fin. While the Forsirovanny (Boosted) logo for the La-5F was round, the FN logo was diamond-shaped.

The La-5FN saw combat for the first time during OPERATION CITADEL, the German offensive around Kursk during the summer of 1943. The arrival of the La-5FN in front line service was a very unpleasant surprise for the Luftwaffe's Luftflotte 4 and 6. Both Luftflotten were heavily committed to providing close air support to the German forces around Kursk. The fourteen La-5FNs of the 32nd Guards Fighter Aviation Regiment took part in 25 aerial engagements during July and August and claimed 33 German aircraft — among them 21 Focke Wulf Fw 190As and three Messerschmitt Bf 109Gs.

The Allies' top ace, Major Ivan N. Kozhedub, claimed his first kills in the La-5 and La-5FN during the Battle of Kursk. During the later Soviet campaign to cross the Dnieper River, Kozhedub quickly scored an additional eleven victories in ten days. His most impressive dis-

Canopy Development

La-5FN Early

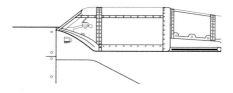

La-5FN Standard

La-5FN Field Modification

Added Grab Handle (Portside Only)

Added Canopy Frame

This early production La-5FN (white 15) was flown by Captain P. J. Likholetov of the 159th Fighter Aviation Regiment, 275th Fighter Aviation Division, 13th Air Army. The inscription on the fuselage reads 'For Vasek and Zhora'. Captain Likholetov achieved a total of 25 personal and 5 shared aerial victories. (Carl-Fredrik Geust)

play of skill came in 1944 over Rumania where he downed eight German aircraft in one week. Kozhedub flew no less than 330 combat missions and took part in 120 engagements in which he claimed 62 victories. He was awarded the title 'Hero of the Soviet Union' three times — the first time on 4 February 1944 as a Senior Lieutenant and a Squadron Commander in the 240th Fighter Aviation Regiment, 5th Air Army after he had shot down 20 enemy aircraft. The second award came on 19 August 1944 after he had scored 34 kills and was a Captain and a Deputy Commander of the 176th Guards Fighter Aviation Regiment, 16th Air Army. His third award came on 18 August 1945 after he was promoted to Major and was still serving as the deputy commander of the 176th Guards Fighter Aviation Regiment. Besides Kozhedub, only one other Soviet pilot, was awarded 'Hero of the Soviet Union' three times with the Golden Star. He was Aleksandr I. Pokryshkin, flying a Lend-Lease Bell P-39 Airacobra. Ivan N. Kozhedub remained in the Air Force and, in 1961, became a Deputy Commander of the Air Force in the Moscow Military District. In 1985, at age of 65, he became a Marshall of the Soviet Union.

During 1943 a total of 5048 La-5F and La-5FN fighters were produced by four State Aircraft Factories in the Soviet Union. Ninety-one percent of the 1943 production (4619 fighters) was built at GAZ-21 at Nizhny-Novgorod. GAZ-381 in Yaroslav built 240 while 184 La-5F and FNs were assembled at GAZ-99 at Ulan Ude. Only five aircraft were built at GAZ-31 in Tbilisi.

During 1944, 3826 La-5FNs were produced in three State Aircraft Factories. GAZ-21 produced 3503, GAZ-381 assembled 221, and GAZ-99 built 102. La-5FN production was gradually phased out as the new La-7 began to leave the assembly lines during April of 1944. The La-5FN and La-7 were produced in parallel until FN production was halted in November of 1944. By then a total of 9920 La-5s had been produced in a number of variants.

The La-5FN did not last very long after the war for a number of reasons. First and foremost

This La-5FN is unusual in that it has an additional vertical frame in the aft sliding canopy. These panels were manufactured in the repair shops. Only a few Lavochkins were fitted with these replacement canopies. (Ivan Ivanov)

Soviet and Bulgarian pilots and ground personnel talk at Kazanlir airfield in Bulgaria during the fall of 1944. The La-5FN behind them is assigned to the 17th Army in support of the 3rd Ukrainian Front. The fighter carries a white rudder, but is otherwise wearing the standard camouflage and markings for the period. (Stephan Boshniakov)

Capt Aleksandr V. Lobanov (left) and Hero of the Soviet Union Guards Maj Aleksandr G. Pavlov stand in front of an La-5FN on 10 April 1945. Both pilots belonged to the 41st Guards FAR, 8th Guards FA Division, 5th Air Army. Captain Lobanov scored 11 kills, while Major Pavlov was credited with 10 kills. The red heart on the cowl is outlined in white. (Ivan Ivanov)

was it was simply obsolete and had been replaced by newer variants of the La-7. Additionally, jet aircraft were also beginning to make themselves felt. Perhaps the greatest reason had to do with the speed at which they were produced. The wooden airframe was simply not designed for a long term use. The La-5 was developed in conditions of total war, and its calculated combat life was shorter than its mechanical life. As a result the La-5's wooden components were not treated with chemicals designed to inhibit rot. Rot and wood fungi began to damage the wooden parts of the aircraft making them unsafe to fly over a long period of time.

Armor Glass

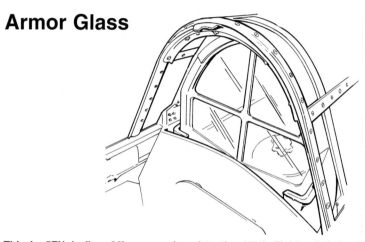

Antenna Lead

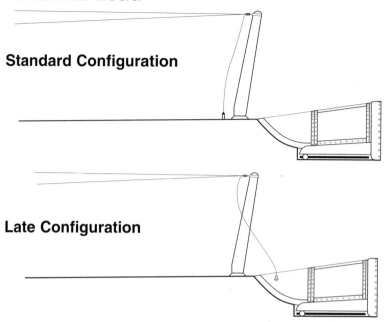

Standard Configuration

Late Configuration

This La-5FN (yellow 36) was assigned to the 159th Fighter Aviation Regiment, 275th Fighter Aviation Division of the 13th Air Army. The aircraft carries a non standard tactical number applied in front of the national marking versus behind as on standard La-5FNs. The unusual insignia is outlined in yellow and red. The rudder, apart from the trim tab, is also painted yellow. A lend-lease C-47 is parked in the background. (Ivan Ivanov)

These late production La-5FNs of the 2nd Guards Fighter Aviation Regiment, 322 Fighter Aviation Division are lined up on their field. The aircraft in the foreground is equipped with a late type antenna configuration with the antenna wire leading into an insulator in the starboard side of the rear canopy. (Ivan Ivanov)

A formation of Czechoslovak La-5FNs cruise in a loose formation while undergoing their conversion training at Kubinka Air Base. White 3 in the background has a broad white band around the aft fuselage. (Ladislav Valousek)

This La-5FN is carrying an AO-25M fragmentation bomb on a D3-40 bomb rack. The AO-25M weighed approximately 25kg (55 lbs) and had a 3.1kg (6.8 lbs) explosive warhead. The AO-25M was equipped with an extended AV-4 fuse which allowed the bomb to detonate above the ground. The inlets in the fuselage exhaust shield are a standard feature of the La-5FN. (Ladislav Valousek)

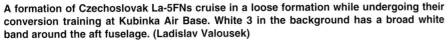

The pilot of La-5FN (white 99) is about to climb aboard his aircraft. The white square on the rudder is a temporary fabric patch. Paint was not always immediately available on the forward airstrips where the fighters normally operated against the Luftwaffe. (Andrzej Morgala)

A late production La-5FN of the 41st Guards Fighter Aviation Regiment, 5th Air Army is readied for a mission during early 1945. The ASh-82FN engine was closely cowled. The vanes behind the spinner were variable to permit additional cooling air into the cowl. The Hucks type start dog protrudes through the spinner. (Ivan Ivanov)

(Below) This La-5FN (white 39) is being readied for a mission while parked on Polish airstrip. The fuel tank cap on the upper wing surface is open and the cut trees used to camouflage the aircraft have been laid to one side. This is a late production La-5FN with the wire leading into the port side of the aft canopy glazing. The fighter is also equipped with the D3-40 bomb racks. (Andrzej Morgala)

(Above) Late production La-5FNs were fitted with an additional, semi-circular access hatch in the lower cowl. All of these aircraft have yellow spinners and rudders. (Ivan Ivanov)

La-5FN Cowling Development

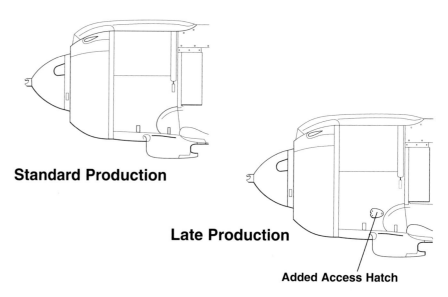

Standard Production

Late Production

Added Access Hatch

La-5 (White 60) of the 159th Fighter Aviation Regiment. The inscription reads, 'Eskadrilja Valerij Chkalov' (Valerij Chkalov Squadron). The aircraft is camouflaged in the early black-green and olive green scheme.

This La-5 flew with the 'Aleksandra Chekalina Squadron' during the winter of 1942 - 1943. The tactical number has been overpainted by a scruffy coat of white camouflage paint.

This La-5F (White 14) was donated by a jazz band led by Leonid Utesov. The inscription reads, 'From the Jazz Band of L. Utesov'. The aircraft is painted in a grey and grey-green camouflage scheme.

The Germans captured this La-5F on the Southern Front. The Aircraft received full Luftwaffe markings over the Russian camouflage. The Balkenkreuz was painted on the upper and lower surfaces of the wings.

White 15 was an early production La-5FN assigned to the 159th Fighter Aviation Regiment. The aircraft is painted using the new camouflage colors of dark grey and light grey. The inscription reads, 'For Vasek and Zhora'

Монгольюкий АРАТ

La-5FN (White 52) was assigned to the 2nd Guards Fighter Aviation Regiment. The inscription reads, 'Mongolskij Arat' and indicated the the fighter was presented by the Mongolian People's Republic.

RENE

La-5FN (White 13) was flown by Pilot Officer Pavel Kocfelda of the 1st Czechoslovak Fighter Regiment. The name 'RENE' refers to Kocfelda's British girlfriend whom he met while serving with the RAF. This aircraft was destroyed during a forced landing at Zolna, Slovakia on 11 October 1944.

Горьковский рабочий

La-7 (White 64) was handed over to the Czech Air Force. The inscription behind the rear canopy reads, 'Workers of Gorkiy' indicating the aircraft was built at State Aircraft Factory 21. This fighter crash landed while in Czech service and was subsequently written off.

La-7 (Yellow 06) carries an unusual camouflage of overall green-grey on the upper surfaces and a non-standard tactical number. Yellow 06 was a later production La-7 armed with three 20mm B-20 cannons.

PL-02

This La-7 was armed with three B-20 cannons and served with the Czech Air Force at Olomouc-Holice airfield in Czechoslovakia during the mid 1950s. The aircraft, designated S-97 in Czech service, carries brown-green upper surfaces over pale blue under-surfaces.

La-5FNs in Foreign Service

On 31 January 1944 twenty highly experienced Czechoslovakian fighter pilots and one ground staff officer were discharged from the British Royal Air Force and transferred to the Soviet Union. The pilots had been serving in the RAF since the summer of 1940 and were to form the nucleus of an independent Czechoslovak fighter regiment with the command structure of the Soviet Air Force. The men arrived in Moscow in early April of 1944 and were assigned to the 6th Reserve Aviation Brigade at Ivanovo airfield approximately 300 km (185 miles) northeast of Moscow. Their aircraft, 24 brand-new La-5FNs were flown in from State Aircraft Factory 381 at Yaroslav on 13 April 1944. The aircraft were hangared on the airfield until the weather became more favorable for the first training flights.

When the training course started on 3 May 1944 each Czechoslovak pilot flew five 30 minute flights in an La-5UTI. They were then considered ready to solo in their La-5FNs. During the training course, the twenty Czechoslovak airmen were augmented by two Slovak pilots, Master Sergeant Anton Matusek and First Sergeant Ludovit Dobrovodsky, who had defected with their Bf 109G-4 fighters on 9 September 1943.

On 18 May 1944 the Czechoslovak pilots transferred from Ivanovo airfield to Kubinka in the southwestern outskirts of Moscow where their conversion training was completed. Each pilot had accumulated 12 hours in the La-5FN. The 1st Czechoslovak Fighter Regiment, as the unit was now designated, was ready for operations at the front.

On 29 August 1944 the Germans began to occupy the territory of its unreliable Slovak allies from several directions. At the same time the Slovak Army, which had declared itself to be a part of the Czechoslovak Army fighting alongside the Allies, began to resist the German incursions. By October of 1944 the insurgent army numbered approximately 50,000 troops and 7,000 partisans. The small insurgent air force was concentrated at Tri Duby (Three Oaks) airfield, lying between Zvolen and Banska Bystrica. The area controlled by the insurgent army was completely surrounded by German forces and was a large, but isolated pocket deep inside German-held territory.

The commander of the insurgent army, General Jan Golian, requested assistance from the Russians. At the time the 1st Czechoslovak Fighter Regiment was based at Proskurov airfield, near Lvov (Lemberg) in the Ukraine and was part of the Soviet 2nd Air Army under the command of General Stepan A. Krasovskij. The Czechoslovak pilots were directed to support the insurgents. On 17 September 1944 the regiment, equipped with 21 La-5FN fighters, landed at the newly built Zolna airfield near Zvolen. During the night the ground staff, fuel, and ammunition were ferried in by Soviet Lisunov Li-2s and Lend-Lease Douglas C-47s.

The 1st Czechoslovak Fighter Regiment was in action the day after their arrival. Eight La-5FNs led by Josef Stehlik attacked the Luftwaffe airfield at Piestany and destroyed 10 aircraft and damaged at least 15 others on the ground without loss. During a US 15th Air Force bombing mission to Bratislava, Slovakia on 20 September 1944, the regiment strafed the airfield of Malacky-Novy-Dvor and prevented the Luftwaffe fighters from intercepting the bombers on their way to the target. During this mission, the Lavochkins destroyed an additional 27 enemy aircraft on the ground. These massive attacks, well behind the Eastern Front, caught the Germans by surprise. As a result the Germans withdrew Schlachtgeschwader 77 from the front in Southern Poland and Jagdgeschwader 52 from Hungary in order to engage the Czech fighter regiment.

The principal mission of the 1st Czechoslovak Fighter Regiment was to provide close air support of the Slovakian insurgent forces. The Regiment attacked German artillery positions, armor, and transports using a pair of 25kg or 50kg (55 lbs or 110 lbs) bombs on the wing racks.

La-5FN (white 20) (foreground) was assigned to Pilot Officer Tomas Motycka. White 69 was flown by Pilot Officer Ladislav Valousek. Both aircraft are being readied for the ferry flight from Proskurov (near Lvov), Ukraine to Krosno on 11 September 1944. (Ladislav Valousek)

The fighters also strafed advancing troops. Due to its vulnerability to ground fire, the La-5FN was ill-suited to these types of missions. Nevertheless, the attacks continued and when the night resupply flights were grounded due to fog, the bomb racks were modified to use Czech made 50kg bombs found in an old ammunition store.

When the fuel supply dwindled, locally available low octane fuel was combined with American 1-TS and Soviet R-9 chemical additives in order to boost the fuel's octane rating to 90. The trials were less than successful when, after 30 to 40 minutes of flight time, the fuel fil-

Tomas Motycka of the 1st Czechoslovak Fighter Regiment sits in his La-5FN (white 20) at Krosno airfield on 17 September 1944. A few minutes later the unit flew to Zolna airfield near Zvolen to provide air support to the insurgents during the Slovakian uprising. Motycka was later killed in action near Diviaky, Slovakia on 15 October 1944. (Ladislav Valousek)

Two La-5FNs prepare to take off from Brezno nad Hronom airfield for a strike on German positions near Jalna on 7 October 1944. When these aircraft returned from their mission, they were attacked by P-51 Mustangs of the 52nd Fighter Group, 15th Air Force. The American pilots mistook the Lavochkins for German Fw 190s. (Ladislav Valousek)

ters clogged and the engine's power fell off rapidly. Keeping the La-5FN in horizontal flight, let alone in combat, became difficult.

On 7 October 1944 an unfortunate incident occurred over Tri Duby. Six B-17Gs from the 483rd Bomb Group, 15th Air Force departed southern Italy to collect American airmen at Tri Duby. The US airmen had been shot down over Slovakia and had been rescued by local inhab-

La-5FN (white 13) was normally flown by Pilot Officer Pavel Kocfelda and named RENE after his British girlfriend. Here, Pilot Officer Vendl, another pilot who occasionally flew the aircraft stands next to the cockpit. This La-5FN is unusual in that it has the antenna lead running from the mast into the port side of the rear canopy. It normally led into the starboard rear canopy. White 13 was destroyed in a forced landing at Zolna on 11 October 1944. (Ladislav Valousek)

itants and partisans. The bombers were escorted by 32 P-51 Mustangs from the 52nd Fighter Group, 15th Air Force. The commander, Lt Col Charles Boedeker, identified an approaching formation of four La-5FNs as Focke Wulf Fw 190s and engaged them. A Lavochkin flown by Sub-Lieutenant Frantisek Sticka was slightly damaged.

The local superiority of the German forces on the ground gradually forced the insurgent units to retreat and the territory under their control rapidly decreased in size. Poor weather halted the aerial combat operations over the territory as well as the resupply bridge from Italy and the USSR. It was soon clear that the uprising was nearing its end. On 25 October 1944 units of the German Kampfgruppe Schill approached Zvolen and forced the evacuation of nearby Tri Duby airfield. Damaged aircraft of the Insurgent Air Force and the 1st Czechoslovak Fighter Regiment, among them some Letov S-328s, a Messerschmitt Bf-109G, a North American P-51 Mustang, as well the two La-5FNs (white 02 and white 58), were burned on the airfield. Despite the poor weather the remaining eleven La-5FNs of the 1st Czechoslovak Fighter Regiment took off in the hope of reaching airstrips behind the Soviet lines. Master Sergeant Anton Matusek was shot down by German Flak over the Dukla pass in the Carpathian mountains, but was hidden by Slovak civilians and subsequently joined the partisans. The remaining ten La-5FNs landed on airstrips in liberated Hungary, Romania, and the Ukraine. Two La-5FNs (s/n 39 21 21 19/white 19 and s/n 39 21 21 24/white 24) were damaged beyond repair when they force landed in Romania.

During its month of operations in Slovakia, the 1st Czechoslovak Fighter Regiment flew 573 sorties and destroyed 13 enemy aircraft — four Bf 109s, three Fi 156 Storch, two Fw 189s, two Fw 190s, and a single Ju 87 and Ju 88. During the ground attack missions two tanks, three anti-aircraft positions, three locomotives, and 77 trucks were destroyed. The unit's own losses included ten La-5FNs destroyed — nearly half the unit. Three pilots, Sublieutenants Frantisek Vaculik, Bohuslav Mraz, and Tomas Motycka, were killed in action. Another pilot, Sublieutenant Jura Reznicek, was seriously wounded. All of the losses were the result of ground fire. Lieutenant Ruda Borovic, a grounded pilot of the 1st Czechoslovak Fighter Regiment, and the chief engineer of the unit, Soviet Sublieutenant Medvedev, joined the partisans after the 1st Czechoslovak Fighter Regiment had evacuated Tri Duby airfield and were subsequently killed by German soldiers while fighting in Slovakia.

On 29 October 1944, shortly after the 1st Czechoslovak Fighter Regiment had returned from Slovakia, Czech Lt Col Ludvik Budin was appointed commander of Czechoslovak flying units in the Soviet Union. He began to build a mixed flying division composed of two La-5 Fighter Regiments and an Il-2 Stormovik Assault Regiment within the command structure of the Soviet 2nd Air Army. The new division was subordinated to the 1st Czechoslovak Army Corps under the command of General Ludvik Svoboda.

The *1. Ceskoslovenska Samostatna Snisena Letecka Divize* (1st Czechoslovak Independent Combined Air Division) was officially formed on 25 January 1945 and transferred to the 8th Air Army under the command of Lieutenant General V. N. Zhdanov. During the final Soviet attacks in 1945 the 8th Air Army provided air support for the 4th Ukrainian Front's offensive through southern Poland and Czechoslovakia — drives that culminated in the capture of Prague.

After completing additional training at Przemysl airfield, Poland the 1st Fighter Regiment was transferred to Poremba airfield — about 20km (12.4 miles) from the front line. On 14 April 1945 the regiment flew its first combat mission. A group of eight Il-2 Type 3 Stormoviks, escorted by nine Czech-flown La-5FNs, attacked artillery positions and tank concentrations near the village of Olza. The mission was part of a Red Army offensive designed to throw the Germans out of the heavily industrialized area of Ostrava in Czechoslovakia. During operations against *Heeresgruppe Mitte*, the La-5FNs of the 1st Fighter Regiment were mainly used in the escort role for the Il-2 Stormoviks of the 3rd Czechoslovak Battle Regiment. On 20 April 1945 the unit lost its last pilot when 1st Lt Michal Minka crashed into a parked Il-2 Stormovik while taking off. During its operations the La-5FNs of the 1st Fighter Regiment had damaged a Messerschmitt Bf 109 and a Focke Wulf Fw 190 and had lost two Lavochkins before the war ended.

Due to lack of La-5FN fighters, the 2nd Fighter Regiment was only able to accomplish their training by using fighters borrowed from the Soviet 41st Fighter Aviation Regiment based at Przemysl. The war in Europe ended before the 2nd Fighter Regiment could be committed to combat.

After the war 31 Lavochkin La-5FNs and La-5UTIs were incorporated into the inventory of the newly formed Czechoslovak Air Force (CAF). Czechoslovakia became the sole operator of the La-5FN outside of the Soviet Union.

In the CAF the La-5FNs were designated S-95 (S for *Stihacka* [Fighter]). These aircraft remained in use after the type had been withdrawn from Soviet service. The Soviet Union had guaranteed an airframe life of two years starting from the date of delivery from the factory. Any operational use of the aircraft beyond this limit required a thorough overhaul. Since the La-5FN had been withdrawn from Soviet service, however, the general overhaul and maintenance facilities no longer existed in the Soviet Union. In July of 1946 a commission of Soviet specialists declared all but two La-5s non-airworthy and directed the aircraft be scrapped. This meant a massive loss of CAF fighter strength, especially since an order for 60 La-7s had not been filled.

Another group of Czechoslovak Air Force and civilian specialists was tasked to examine the La-5 safety question and they reached more favorable conclusion, only recommending a ban on aerobatics in some of the aircraft. Despite the group's recommendations, an La-5FN and La-5UTI were subjected to a series of static tests at the Scientific Aviation Institute at Letnany. The results were not favorable as it was found that the tensile and bending strength of the plywood was only 50 percent when compared to the original specifications. All of the CAF Lavochkins were grounded on 13 December 1946.

A further study by the Scientific Aviation Institute revealed that the poor quality of the plywood had already been calculated into the airframe static equations. The design had even catered for maintaining the fighter's airworthiness while the fuselage shell was slightly damaged. Structural defects discovered in the fuselage and the tail sections were caused by the unnecessarily stiff tail wheel shock absorbers which transmitted too many landing forces to the tail structure, especially during hard landings. These discoveries confirmed the great care expended by the Lavochkin Design Bureau to produce a durable airframe — even when using poor quality materials and built under crude conditions in relocated factories.

The conclusions made by the Scientific Aviation Institute permitted the reinstatement of the La-5FN and La-5UTI into service during 1947. By 1 July 1948 the Czechoslovak Air Force had 23 La-5FN and La-5UTI aircraft on strength. By the end of 1948, however, most La-5FNs had reached the end of their life and were gradually withdrawn from service use.

The Czechoslovak La-5FN's upper surfaces were repainted overall green-grey, while the under surfaces were painted in light blue. The Czechoslovak Air Force insignia consisted of a large red, white, and blue trisected disk outlined in white. The insignia was applied to the vertical fin and the upper and lower wing surfaces. At first, the aircraft retained their two-digit white tactical number on the fuselage, but these were gradually replaced by a black three digit/letter code on the fuselage and the wing under surfaces.

La-5FN (white 12) of the 1st Czechoslovak Fighter Regiment takes off from Tri Duby (Three Oaks) airfield during the Slovak uprising. White 12 was another aircraft unable to return to Soviet lines after the end of the operation. It was destroyed to keep it out of German hands. The canopy was usually open for taxiing and takeoff to allow a rapid evacuation in an emergency. (Ladislav Valousek)

Polish La-5FN

Poland received a single La-5FN in 1945 when the Polish Air Force briefly considered equipping some of their Fighter Aviation Regiments with the La-5FN. The idea was soon discarded and the Yakovlev Yak-9P was chosen as the standard fighter for the Polish Air Force. No flight trials were ever performed. The aircraft is believed to have been scrapped sometime in 1949.

La-5FN (s/n 39 21 21 24/white 24) is being towed across the airfield after heavy rains softened the field. This aircraft was written off when it crash-landed in Romania after evacuating Tri Duby on 25 October 1944. (Ladislav Valousek)

La-5FNs line up at Przemysl airfield, Poland on 7 November 1944 after the 1st Czechoslovak Fighter Regiment had returned from their operations in Slovakia. La-5FN (serial number 39 20 34 53/white 53) was assigned to the unit as a replacement. The aircraft subsequently saw post-war service with the Czechoslovak Air Force. (Ladislav Valousek)

This La-5FN (white 88) was written off after newly trained Sergeant Diacuk crash-landed at Przemysl airfield, Poland on 6 December 1944. It was one of the Lavochkins that flew combat operations from Tri Duby airfield behind the German lines in Slovakia. The aircraft had survived to return to Soviet lines only to be destroyed by an inexperienced pilot during a training flight. (Ladislav Valousek)

Squadron Leader Frantisek Fajtls flew La-5FN (white 58). The aircraft had a red cowl ring and a red spinner with a black tip which indicated the aircraft's assignment to the commander of the 1st Czechoslovak Fighter Regiment. On 25 October 1944 the aircraft was burned at Tri Duby airfield to keep it from falling into German hands when the airfield was being evacuated. (Ladislav Valousek)

The war is over and a group of Czech pilots have their picture taken in front of an La-5FN (white 31) at Balice airfield near Krakow, Poland on 9 May 1945. The spinner is painted red with a white spiral — a design often used on German fighters. The next day, white 31 was transferred to the 10th Training Aviation Regiment. (Ladislav Valousek)

La-5FNs and La-7s line up at Letnany Airfield near Prague, Czechoslovakia on 1 June 1945. During the ceremonial display the President of Czechoslovakia, Dr. Edvard Benes, passed the operational standard of the 1st Czechoslovak Mixed Air Division to the commanding officer of the division, Colonel Ludvik Budin. (Zdenek Hurt)

After the war, the Czechoslovak La-5FNs gradually received a grey-green camouflage scheme over the upper surfaces of the aircraft. The Czechoslovak national markings replaced the original red and white star of the Soviet Air Force. (Zdenek Titz)

La-5FNs sit on the flight line at Praha-Kbely Air Force Base, Czechoslovakia during 1946. The near aircraft carries a white spinner. The third aircraft in line (s/n 39 21 21 17/ white 17) was an original Lavochkin assigned to the Czechoslovaks in April of 1944. It saw extensive action at Tri Duby, Slovakia. (Bohumir Kudlicka)

A Czechoslovak La-5FN runs up its engine during a test. The aircraft has received the new grey-green upper surface camouflage, but still lacks a tactical number on the rear fuselage. (Andrzej Morgala)

Lavochkin La-5 '206'

The La-5FN was the first Soviet fighter with performance that was superior to the Messerschmitt Bf 109G. The Shvetsov design team, however, realized that the advantage would be short-lived. They also came to the conclusion that it was not possible to increase the power of the ASh-82FN engine much beyond the 1850 hp the powerplant already provided. Additionally, there were no other radial engines in development that held the promise of superior performance to the ASh-82FN. For a brief time the 2200 hp ASh-71F engine had been regarded a potential successor, but the engine proved to be so unreliable that its use was out of the question.

The only viable alternatives to a new engine were additional weight reductions and careful refinements of the La-5FN's aerodynamics. The weight reduction program, replacing wooden parts with light metal alloy parts, was largely accomplished on the production line beginning with late production La-5F and continuing through the production of the La-5FN.

By 1943 an La-5 had already undergone a series of tests in the huge T-104 wind tunnel at the Central Aero Hydrodynamics Institute (TsAGI) in Zhukovsky. The tests revealed that simply sealing the gaps in the airframe would gain an additional 24 kmh (14.9 mph) in speed. Further tests indicated another six kmh (3.7 mph) would be available if the main wheel wells were fully covered. Another test relocated the oil cooler from under the nose to a position underneath the fuselage. Parasitic drag was reduced by 50 percent while the flow of air through the cooler was increased by 35 percent.

The results were impressive enough to warrant further testing on a standard production

The La-5 '206' was the result of an attempt to institute aerodynamic refinements into the La-5FN design. As a result of extensive wind tunnel testing, changes were made to the spinner, engine cowling, supercharger intake trunking, oil cooler, and the radio antenna arrangement. Although the La-5 '206' did not see operational service, many of the refinements were incorporated into the later La-7. (Yefim Gordon)

La-5FN (s/n 39 21 02 06). Aside from making the refinements noted above, the aircraft had its spinner enlarged and the Hucks starter dog eliminated. The aircraft, now known as the La-5 '206', also received a broader, single piece cowling. The exhaust cover plates were reduced in size and squared off while the three small louvers at the rear of the exhaust shields were deleted.

The supercharger intake trunk fairing was moved to the underside of the cowling. This forced the location of the oil cooler further aft to a position under the fuselage even with the wing trailing edge. The oil cooler's housing was also slightly modified. The dural fuselage side panels added to the La-5FN fuselage were deleted — a measure that resulted in less drag. The fresh air inlets in front of the canopy were deleted, as was the radio mast. The wire antennas now ran from the leading edge of the vertical fin to a pair of small blisters located behind the rear canopy fairing. A new main wheel well door was added to the La-5 '206' which completely sealed the wheel well. This modification also resulted in less drag.

Between 16 December 1943 and 10 February 1944 the La-5 '206' was evaluated under the direction of N. V. Adamovich at the Flight Research Institute at Zhukovsky Air Base. The flight tests confirmed the calculations of the TsAGI. The La-5 '206' had a top speed at sea level of 630 kmh (391 mph). At 6150 meters (20,177 feet) the top speed rose to 684 kmh (425 mph) — 50 kmh (31 mph) faster than a standard production La-5FN. This was accomplished even though the La-5 '206', at a take off weight of 3445 kg (7594 lbs), was approximately 150 kg (330 lbs) heavier than a standard La-5FN.

Ultimately, none of the aerodynamic refinements were incorporated into production La-5FNs. The La-5 '206' program, however, provided a wealth of valuable data that aided in the development of future Soviet fighters, most notably the upcoming La-7.

La-5FN/La-5 '206' Development

La-5FN

La-5 '206'

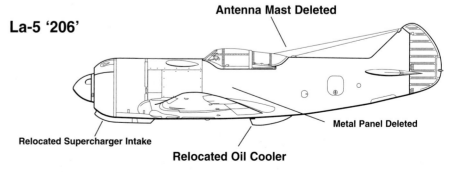

Antenna Mast Deleted

Metal Panel Deleted

Relocated Supercharger Intake

Relocated Oil Cooler

Lavochkin La-5FN (Model 1944)

The La-5 '206' was a project under the control of the scientists of the Central Aero Hydrodynamics Institute. Their goal had been to improve the aerodynamics of the La-5FN airframe, but they did not look into the feasibility of incorporating the improvements into production fighters. The Lavochkin Design Bureau, using shared research data, took over this portion of the project. During January of 1944 construction of a new variant, initially designated the La-5FN Model 1944, was completed by the Lavochkin Design Bureau at State Aircraft Factory 21 at Nizhny-Novgorod. Nearly all of the aerodynamic changes recommended by the TsAGI were introduced. The aircraft served as a pattern aircraft for the La-7 project and only a single prototype was built.

The La-5FN Model 1944 reintroduced the standard spinner of the La-5FN as well as the use of a radio mast to support the antenna wires, although the mast was slightly slimmer. The new locations of the oil cooler and supercharger intake were retained from the '206', but the supercharger intake trunk was only slightly modified. Most of the changes found on the La-5F '206' ultimately found their way into the La-7.

The La-5FN Model 1944 represented an attempt to incorporate some of the aerodynamic improvements of the La-5 '206' into a production aircraft. The La-5FN Model 1944 reintroduced the standard spinner and radio antenna arrangement of the La-5FN. The program was terminated in favor of the more highly refined La-7 (Ivan Ivanov)

La-5 '206'/La-5FN (Model 1944) Development

La-5 '206'

La-5FN (Model 1944)

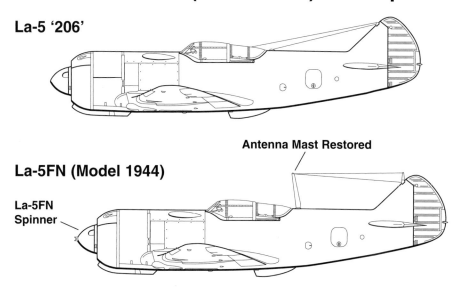

Antenna Mast Restored

La-5FN Spinner

Lavochkin La-5 'M-71'

In early 1943, the Lavochkin Design Bureau began an alternative engine program for the La-5. Great hope was placed on the new ASh-71F (F for Forsirovanny [Boosted]) twin row, air-cooled radial engine. The 2200 hp engine was intended to replace the ASh-82FN engine on the La-5FN. With almost 350 hp more than the ASh-82FN powerplant, the engine would dramatically improve the performance of the La-5FN.

The design of the ASh-71F had begun in 1940 by joining a pair of nine-cylinder M-63 engines to form a single 18-cylinder twin row radial engine with direct fuel injection. Of interest, the M-63 was an improved copy of the American Wright Cyclone R-1820 G-5 engine. With all of the engine mounted accessories attached, the ASh-71F weighed 1556 kg (3430 lbs).

The first examples of the ASh-71 provided 2000 hp at take off — nearly twice the power of the Klimov M-105 in-line piston engines used to power the LaGG-3 and Yak-1 fighters. At an altitude of 2600 meters (8530 feet) the ASh-71 was rated at 1800 hp and at 6250 meters (20,502 feet) the engine was still developing a remarkable 1670 hp. Nevertheless, severe teething troubles delayed the engine's introduction into front line service and the first engines were not available until early 1942.

While still in development, an ASh-71 engine was installed into a prototype Polikarpov I-185 fighter in March of 1941, but the aircraft did not fly until February of 1942. The I-185 had been developed as a competitive design to the La-5FN and flew up to 680 kmh (422 mph) during the factory test trials. By January of 1943 the NKAP decided that further development of the I-185 should be postponed since it was clear that the La-5FN was better suited for the Soviet Air Force. Combat evaluations using a number of I-185 prototypes assigned to the 18th Guards Fighter Aviation Regiment on the Kalinin Front clearly demonstrated that the ASh-71 was mechanically unreliable. The I-185 also used large quantities of duralumin in its airframe — an alloy in short supply.

The development of the ASh-71F powered version of the La-5 was conducted in parallel with the La-5FN and ASh-82FN engine at the Lavochkin Design Bureau. The ASh-71F engine was

The La-5 ASh-71F was an attempt to incorporate a more powerful radial engine into the La-5F airframe. The larger, 2200 hp, 18 cylinder ASh-71F engine required a broader cowling. The engine proved to be unreliable and the program was terminated. (Ivan Ivanov)

mounted into an La-5 airframe that had also been modified with some of the attributes of the La-5F, most notably the cut down rear fuselage and full canopy. Additionally, a number of the aerodynamic refinements tested on the La-5 '206' also found their way onto the La-5 ASh-71F airframe. These included the broad chord, single piece cowling, the supercharger intake mounted under the nose, and the relocation of the oil cooler to the lower fuselage even with the wing trailing edge. The La-5 ASh-71F also lacked the dural panels on the fuselage side and, at 8.31 meters (27.26 feet) long, was slightly shorter than the 8.67 meter (28.4 feet) long La-5F/5FN. The wings were unchanged, but the wheel wells were completely enclosed by flush fitting doors. With a take-off weight of 3,516 kg (7751 lbs), the ASh-71F powered prototype was 358 kg (789 lbs) heavier than the contemporary La-5FN.

The La-5 ASh-71F prototype was painted in the standard camouflage pattern of black-green and olive green upper surfaces over light blue lower surfaces with the national insignia — a red star with black edging — applied on the rear fuselage, tail, and lower wing surfaces. The spinner was painted yellow.

The La-5 ASh-71F took off for its maiden flight on 28 April 1943 — only a few weeks after the La-5FN prototype flew for the first time. Between late April and June of 1943 the aircraft was tested at the Scientific Research Institute of the Soviet Air Force at Sverdlovsk. The initial figures were promising. The fighter had a top speed at sea level of 612 kmh (380 mph) and a speed of 685 kmh (425 mph) at 5500 meters (18,044 feet). The speeds were 50 kmh and 37 kmh (31 and 22.9 mph) higher than those of the ASh-82FN powered La-5. However, the overall performance of the ASh-71F powered prototype did not meet the expectations of the Lavochkin Design Bureau and the NKAP. It was then decided to take the La-5 ASh-71F to the Central Aero Hydrodynamics Institute (TsAGI) where it was tested in the full scale T-104 wind tunnel. The camouflage paint was stripped off the airframe for these tests.

The root cause of the performance deficiency was found in the poor production finish, particularly in the engine cowling, which caused the aerodynamic drag to be far greater than expected. The engineers in the TsAGI concluded that once the corrective measures where introduced, the La-5 with the ASh-71F engine could attain a maximum speed of about 720 kmh (447 mph).

The aircraft still failed to prove itself, however, due to the unreliable engine. It soon became clear that the ASh-71F would never enter full scale production because its shortcomings would never be completely solved by the Shvetsov Design Bureau. Further development of the La-5 ASh-71F was terminated. Only a limited number of ASh-71 engines were built and these were used experimentally in Polikarpov and Lavochkin fighters.

With La-5 ASh-71F testing at a dead end, the reliable ASh-82FN was chosen as the standard twin-row radial engine of the Soviet Air Force's fighters and bombers — a position it held until the end of the Great Patriotic War.

La-5 M-71/ASh-71

New Engine and Cowling

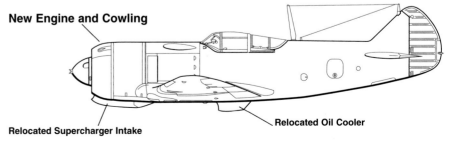

Relocated Supercharger Intake

Relocated Oil Cooler

Lavochkin La-5UTI

During the summer of 1943 a two-seat trainer variant based on the La-5F was developed by the Lavochkin Design Bureau. The La-5UTI (UTI=*Uchebno Trenirovochny Istrebitel* [Fighter Trainer]) was a straight forward adaptation of the single-seat Lavochkin with a second cockpit for the instructor inserted aft of the radio bay. The instructor was provided with duplicate flight controls and the front cockpit controls were automatically disconnected whenever the instructor took control. Both cockpits were enclosed by two aft-sliding canopies. The trainer retained the fuselage length and ASh-82F engine of the La-5F fighter.

In keeping with its non-combatant training role, the La-5UTI dispensed with many features found on the combat fighter — many deleted simply to save weight. The armor glass behind the windscreen, the armor glass behind the pilot's head, and the seat back armor were eliminated. The wing fuel tank fire suppression system which ducted cold, inert exhaust gases into the wing fuel tanks was deleted as well. The small cockpit air inlets in front of the canopy on the La-5F/FN were deleted on the La-5UTI trainer version.

The La-5UTI lacked any provision for oxygen equipment. No RSI-4 radio was carried on the initial versions of the La-5UTI trainer and, as a result, the associated mast and tail stub were deleted. Since the second cockpit intruded slightly into the space occupied by the wing tanks, there was a slight reduction in fuel.

The La-5UTIs retained a single 20mm ShVAK cannon with 170 rounds of ammunition fitted into the port side of the nose. Both cannon ports and breech fairings found on the single seat La-5 were retained. The guns were sighted using the standard PBP-1B gun sight. All bomb related equipment was deleted. The efforts to save weight were reasonably successful. The trainer's take off weight of 3210 kg (7076 lbs) was nearly identical to that of the single-seat La-5F fighter.

The La-5UTI prototype was tested at the Scientific Research Institute between 3 and 30 September 1943. The trainer had a top speed at sea level of 552 kmh (343 mph)— only 5 kmh (3.1 mph) less than that of the La-5F fighter. The La-5UTI reached its top speed of 600 kmh (372 mph) at an altitude of 3500 meters (11,482 feet) and required 5.7 minutes to climb to 5000 meters (16,404 feet). Overall, the performance and the handling characteristics of the La-5UTI were quite similar to the single-seat La-5F.

The La-5UTI prototype and the first production batches were equipped with an aft sliding rear canopy with a squared off rear frame. Most of the follow-on La-5UTIs were equipped with a new rear canopy with the rear frame slanted to the rear, which provided better visibility for the instructor in the rear cockpit. Early trainers also lacked an external grab handle on the port side of the aft canopy, but this was added to all later aircraft.

The La-5UTI trainers were essentially two-seat modifications of both the La-5F and La-5FN single-seat fighters and shared most of the physical attributes of their fighter counterparts. La-5UTI trainers powered by the ASh-82F engine retained the two piece cowl with external buckles, an air intake in the upper cowl lip, and single exhausts on the fuselage sides. The wings of the ASh-82F powered La-5UTI were produced with wooden main spars and three fuel tanks. Later production aircraft were built with metal sparred wings and four fuel tanks.

When the State Aircraft Factories switched production to the improved La-5FN powered by the ASh-82FN engine, a corresponding change was made in the La-5UTI program. The La-5FN based trainers retained most of the changes introduced on the La-5FN, including the metal sparred wings and four fuel tanks.

The ASh-82FN powered La-5UTIs also introduced the RSI-4 radio system with an aerial wire running from a small stub on the vertical fin to an entry point on the fuselage centerline behind the canopy.

The early La-5UTIs were powered by an ASh-82F engine. These early trainers lacked radio systems and were equipped with a squared off rear canopy over the instructor. (Ivan Ivanov)

The La-5UTIs were allocated to the Training Aviation Regiments, Reserve Aviation Brigades, and Fighter Aviation Regiments serving on the front. Normally a Fighter Aviation Regiment was allocated two to four La-5UTI aircraft for supplemental training and inter-unit liaison duties. The trainer's performance also allowed it to serve in the high speed liaison role.

This La-5UTI (white 100) was converted from a single-seat fighter by the 1st Air Depot at Leningrad. The slanted cross frame in the windscreen indicates the aircraft was an La-5 powered by an ASh-82A engine. This trainer has been equipped with a radio system. (Ivan Ivanov)

La-5UTI production continued well after La-5FN production had ceased at the State Aircraft Factories. Large numbers of La-5UTIs also served in La-7 equipped fighter regiments because the La-7UTI trainers did not become operational until the spring of 1946. Since only a limited number of La-7UTIs were built, the La-5UTI remained the standard trainer for La-5 and La-7 pilots.

The La-5UTIs were delivered with dark-grey and medium grey-green upper surfaces and light blue under surfaces. Late version national insignias were placed on the fuselage sides, vertical fin, and the wing under surface. The white two-digit tactical numbers — the last two digits of the serial number — were applied on the production line and often had a thin red or black outline. The Forsirovanny (Boosted) logo on the ASh-82F powered trainers was applied on both sides of the engine cowling as a yellow disc with a red Cyrillic "F". The yellow disc had a thin red outline. The white 'FN' logos on ASh-82FN powered trainers were applied in the same position. Not all La-5UTIs had the logo applied at the factory and some aircraft had them overpainted at unit level.

A number of La-5, La-5F, and La-5FN single-seat fighters were converted to La-5UTI trainers at special maintenance facilities of the Soviet Air Force. These aircraft shared most of the attributes, including the original engines, of factory built trainers. La-5UTIs that came out of the Maintenance and Repair Facilities had all of the armor removed. Some converted aircraft kept their RSI-4 radios although the radio mast was deleted with the aerial wire running from the fin to the fuselage centerline behind the canopy.

When twenty Czech airmen transferred from the British RAF to the Soviet Air Force began training at Ivanovo airfield in May of 1944, their complement of 24 La-5FN fighters included a single La-5UTI (white 06). The training element of the 1. Ceskoslovenska Samostatna Snisena Letecka Divize (1st Czechoslovak Independent Combined Air Division) operated a single La-5UTI and two Yak-7UTI aircraft during February of 1945. Three additional La-5UTI were allocated to the 1st Fighter Regiment when the unit underwent training at Przemysl airfield in Poland during February of 1945.

After World War II four CS-95, as the La-5UTI was designated in Czechoslovakia, served

La-5UTI Development

La-5UTI (Early)

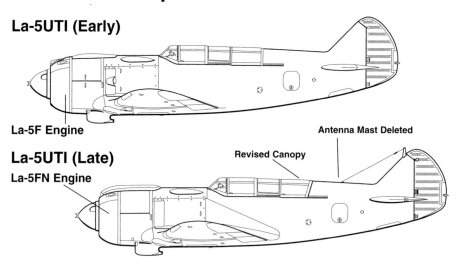

La-5F Engine

Antenna Mast Deleted

La-5UTI (Late)

Revised Canopy

La-5FN Engine

with the Czechoslovak Air Force. All four aircraft were ASh-82FN powered trainers from the late production batches. Czechoslovakia was the sole operator of the Lavochkin trainer outside the Soviet Union. The Czech Air Force made only one modification — removing the tail wheel doors. The trainers were painted and marked in an identical fashion to the fighters.

Although briefly grounded with the Czech Air Force La-5FNs on late 1946, the CS-95s were reinstated into service during 1947 and continued in operations until 1950 when the last surviving aircraft (registration B-4998) was finally withdrawn from service. At the time the aircraft was believed to be the last surviving airworthy La-5 in the world.

At least two La-5UTIs (white 12 and white 17) were assigned to the 1st Fighter Regiment of the 1st Czechoslovak Independent Combined Air Division. White 17 later served in the post-war Czech Air Force. (Ladislav Valousek)

La-5UTI trainers continued to serve in the Czech Air Force during the post-war years. Both aircraft are wearing grey-green camouflaged upper surfaces and the modern Czech Air Force insignia. The tail wheel doors have been removed. (Zdenek Titz)

Lavochkin La-7

During the fall of 1943 it became clear to Arcadiy D. Shvetsov and his design team that it was not possible to increase the power of the ASh-82FN engine beyond its current output of 1850 hp. Additionally there were no other reliable radial engines of superior performance to the ASh-82FN. For a time the 2200 hp ASh-71F was regarded as a promising alternative, however, tests with an ASh-71F equipped La-5 revealed the ASh-71F to be so unreliable that its use was out of the question.

As a result only two alternatives remained for the Lavochkin Design Bureau — a further weight reduction and a careful aerodynamic improvement of the La-5FN. The weight reduction efforts were performed on the production line by exchanging certain wooden parts with light metal parts, however, there were no aerodynamic refinements made to the La-5FN. Instead, the refinements were made to a new version of the basic La-5 airframe designated the La-7. These improvements had been tested on the earlier La-5FN and La-5 '206', both of which had been tested in a wind tunnel by the Central Aero Hydrodynamics Institute (TsAGI) at Zhukovsky. Many of the aerodynamic refinements tested and finalized on the La-5 '206' were introduced on the La-7 prototype. In that regard, the La-5 '206' can be considered the La-7 prototype.

Semyon Mikhailovich Alexeyev, the deputy designer at the Lavochkin Design Bureau, took control of the La-7 project since Lavochkin remained in Moscow. The first purpose-built La-7 prototype was completed in January of 1944. Most of the aerodynamic changes recommended by the TsAGI were incorporated into the prototype's airframe including, at first, the sealing of airframe and cowling gaps both inside and outside the aircraft.

The starter dog was removed from the La-7's spinner on the prototype and all subsequent production versions. The La-7's spinner was also more pointed. The ASh-82FNV engine turned a new VISh-105V-4 propeller which replaced the VISh-105V propeller of the La-5FN. The engine oil cooler was moved from below the cowl to a position under the fuselage even with the wing trailing edge. The long supercharger intake on top of the cowl was removed and replaced by a flush intake in the leading edge of both wing roots. The exhaust outlet cover panel was slightly revised, being both smaller and having a slightly different shape.

The wheel wells were fitted with rectangular doors, however, these were later changed to a triangular shape on the production models. The prototype also shared the same main gear strut doors as the La-5FN, but these were later revised to completely smooth doors on production aircraft. The main gear struts were also lengthened by 80mm (3 inches) compared to the La-5FN.

The fresh air inlets in front of the La-5F and FN canopies were deleted. The cockpit layout was revised and the instrument panel was changed, although the spartan look of the La-5FN cockpit remained. The La-7 still lacked an artificial horizon gauge. Whereas the La-5FN used a spade type control stick, the La-7 used a stick similar to the American fighters — a direct copy of those supplied by the US to the USSR under Lend-Lease. Additionally, refinements to the elevators resulted in reduced control stick forces.

The La-7 prototype lacked the radio antenna mast and aerial stub on the vertical fin, a design element tested on the La-5 '206', but production aircraft received a mast and the standard aerial stub. The new mast was slightly slimmer than the mast used on the La-5s.

On 2 February 1944 test pilot G. M. Shiyanov began the La-7 prototype's flight test program and the results proved to be encouraging. A maximum speed of 597 kmh (371 mph) was recorded at sea level. This was remarkably superior to the La-5FN's speed of 546 kmh (339 mph) and the Focke Wulf Fw-190A-8's speed of 560 kmh (347 mph) at the same altitude.

Two weeks later on 16 February 1944, the La-7 prototype was handed over for State Acceptance Trials. The trials, however, were not without incident. On 20 February 1944 test pilot Major Kubyshkin experienced an inflight engine failure when an engine connecting rod failed and he was forced to make an emergency landing. By 8 March 1944 the engine had been repaired and the testing program was continued.

Most of the testing had been completed by 22 March 1944 when the aircraft suffered a complete failure of the number 12 bulkhead in the aft fuselage while taxiing. The failure was traced to the absence of resin bonding in the joints — a defect that was attributed to poor, and perhaps rushed, assembly. Once again the pilot's skills prevented the aircraft from suffering further damage.

While the first La-7 prototype was being evaluated, a second prototype was completed and became available for additional testing. This aircraft was equipped with a fuselage mounted

The second La-7 prototype reintroduced the antenna mast and aerial stub. The aircraft also features the revised main gear doors, but still lacks doors over the tail wheel well. (Ivan Ivanov)

An early production La-7 is still equipped with the old antenna configuration adopted from the La-5FN. The wire lead ran from the antenna mast to the rear starboard side of the canopy. (Ivan Ivanov)

radio mast and an aerial stub on the vertical fin. Additionally, the shape of the main wheel doors was revised and the two blisters on the doors were deleted leaving the entire door flush with the wing's lower surface. The second airframe also lacked tail wheel doors. Apart from these changes, and a more conical shape to the spinner, the second prototype was virtually identical to the first.

Despite the short term difficulties faced during the La-7 evaluation, the acceptance trials were successfully completed on 27 March 1944. In his flight test report Major Kubyshkin stated that compared with the standard La-5FN, the La-7's rate of climb had improved considerably. A maximum speed of 680 kmh (422 mph) at an altitude of 6000 meters (19,685 feet) was recorded with the La-7 prototype — at the time the best performance for a Soviet fighter. However, the dramatic rise in performance was gained at a cost. At maximum power the cockpit temperature rose to 40° Celsius (104° Fahrenheit) even while operating in the bitter cold of the Russian winter. The temperature rise was caused by the elimination of the cockpit air inlets and poor thermal insulation between the cockpit and engine bay. The situation was worsened by the hot oil lines running between the oil cooler and the engine and passing directly beneath the pilot's feet. Additionally, poor internal sealing allowed exhaust gases to enter the cockpit and the pilots reported the odor of exhaust gases and burning rubber in the cockpit. The lack of proper ventilation also increased the condensation in the cockpit. Test pilots also complained about excessive rudder pedal forces and the absence of an emergency canopy release. These poor operating conditions, even in normal flight, could lead to greatly increased pilot fatigue and a higher accident and combat loss rate.

The list of complaints over the La-7 prototype was long. In addition to poor ventilation, high rudder pedal forces, and lack of an emergency canopy release, complaints were made about the lack of a single control to regulate engine speed and propeller pitch, an automatic supercharger control, and a new cowl flap control system. Such devices were already in use on Germany's Fw 190 where a single lever controlled engine speed and propeller pitch. In the La-7 the pilot had to make up to eight separate movements to properly control engine speed, propeller pitch, and supercharger boost — actions often difficult to accomplish in combat.

A production La-7 (white 50) was tested at the Scientific Research Institute during 1944. This aircraft carries the standard La-7 camouflage of grey and grey-green upper surfaces over light blue under surfaces. The tactical number is thinly outlined in red. (Nigel A. Eastaway/RART)

Regrettably, of the long list of complaints, only two — the automatic propeller pitch change mechanism and a jettisonable canopy — were incorporated into the production La-7. The new fighter was to be rushed into combat as soon as possible.

Production La-7s differed little from the prototype and shared many similarities with the La-5 '206'. Additional hinged panels were incorporated into the cowling to facilitate maintenance. Whereas the La-5FN used a metal holding strap wrapped around the top half of the rear cowl section, the La-7 had the strap wrapped completely around the rear cowl. The three louvers at the rear of the exhaust shield were retained from the La-5FN, but these were smaller. Along the fuselage sides the La-7 received an enlarged, rectangular dural panel versus the triangular type used on the La-5FN. The dural wing root fillet was also strengthened and enlarged on the La-7.

Early La-7s used a radio antenna mast and aerial arrangement similar to the later production La-5FNs. Most La-7s, however, slightly altered the arrangement where the wire ran from the mast into the fuselage. The La-7s also used a mast of smaller cross-section that was not slanted forward as on the La-5FN. A few La-7s were delivered with a slightly shorter mast. After the end of the Great Patriotic War a number of La-7s were equipped with a radio compass. A direction finding loop was placed on top of the fuselage behind the antenna mast.

Most La-7s used the 20mm ShVAK cannons with 200 rounds per gun and PBP-1B gun sight. The spent cartridges were ejected through circular apertures below the fuselage. The last La-7 production batches were equipped with three 20mm Berezin B-20 cannons, a newly designed weapon that entered the Soviet Air Force inventory in 1945. The guns were asymmetrically mounted with two on the port side of the upper fuselage and one on the starboard side. La-7s equipped with the B-20 cannon had three long rectangular bulges over the weapons while the ShVAK cannon equipped aircraft had a pair of tear-drop shaped fairings to cover the gun breeches. The B-20 cannon weighed only 25 kg (55 lbs) when compared to the 42 kg (99 lbs) of a single ShVAK 20mm cannon. Ammunition supply was 150 rounds per gun and the spent shells were ejected through square apertures on the fuselage sides. The ShVAK and B-20 can-

La-7 Development

La-5FN

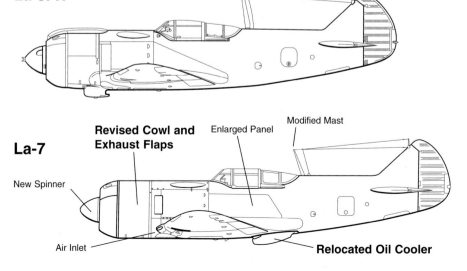

La-7

- New Spinner
- Air Inlet
- **Revised Cowl and Exhaust Flaps**
- Enlarged Panel
- Modified Mast
- **Relocated Oil Cooler**

nons fired the same ammunition which eased the manufacturing and supply situation. La-7s equipped with the B-20 cannons also had the lower of the three louvers on the exhaust shield deleted. La-7s equipped with both weapons could be found flying in the same regiments. By the end of the war in Europe 368 B-20 armed La-7s had been delivered to the front. La-7s were equipped to carry a pair of bomb racks capable of mounting bombs up to 100 kg (220 lbs) although these were rarely carried during ordinary fighter operations.

The La-7 had a fuselage of monocoque construction with pine bulkheads and longerons covered with a stressed skin made of layers of birch plywood. Its thickness was gradually reduced from 6.8mm (.26 inches) to 3.5mm (.13 inches) towards the tail. The fuselage nose section was fabricated from welded Chrome Molybdenum steel tubes. This section included the engine, gun mounts, and attachments for the ammunition boxes and oil tank. The cockpit canopy consisted of tubular framework and perspex glazing. The windscreen was backed by a 55mm (2.16 inch) thick armor glass plate. The center section of the canopy slid aft to permit entry and exit. A red lever on the starboard cockpit wall jettisoned the canopy and its rails in an emergency. Behind the pilot's head was a 66mm (2.59 inches) armor glass plate, while the seat back was protected by a 8.5mm (.33 inches) thick metal plate.

The wing consisted of a center section built integrally with the fuselage and two outer panels. The joints between the center section and the outer panels were covered by dural strips. The wings were built using metal and wood. The two spars were built from angle steel with dural walls and the ribs were assembled using pine strips. The wings were skinned using bakelite plywood ranging in thickness from 2.5mm (.1 inch) to 5mm (.19 inch). The flaps, slats, and ailerons were made from dural. The flaps and slats were skinned with dural sheet, while the ailerons were fabric covered. The space between the spars was taken up by self-sealing fuel tanks equipped with the inert exhaust gas filling system used on the La-5s. Removable plywood panels on the bottom of the wing provided access to the wing fuel tanks.

Landing Gear Development

The main wheels and tail wheels were hydraulically retracted and were completely enclosed by dural covers. In an emergency the gear could be extended pneumatically. The main wheel brakes were pneumatically operated.

The wooden vertical fin was built integrally with the wooden fuselage. The detachable horizontal stabilizers were also made of wood. The rudder and elevators were made from dural and covered with fabric. A system of rods and bellcranks operated the elevators and ailerons, while the rudder was controlled via cables connected to the rudder pedals.

The first production La-7s were equipped with the 1850 hp ASh-82FN engine, but all later production variants were equipped with the ASh-82FNV engine. The engine had the same power rating as the ASh-82FN, but offered improved performance at higher altitudes.

The hand built and finished La-7 prototype had a greatly improved performance over the La-5FN. The performance of production La-7s, however, suffered from their being quickly built on a fast-moving assembly line. Nevertheless, the production La-7's increased performance was still impressive.

The standard production La-7 had a top speed of 592 kmh (367 mph) at sea level — 46 kmh (28.5 mph) more than the La-5FN and 72 kmh (44.7 mph) more than the Focke Wulf Fw 190A-3. The improved performance was due to the aerodynamic refinements of the airframe and a weight reduction of some 82 kg (180 lbs). At 6100 meters (20,000 feet) the La-7 had a top speed of 655 kmh (407 mph), 35 kmh (21.7 mph) more than the La-5FN. The La-7 was also 15 kmh (9 mph) faster than the Focke Wulf Fw 190A-8, the latest version of this German fighter deployed to the Eastern Front. With a take off weight of 3240 kg (7142 lbs), the La-7 was about 1060 kg (2336 lbs) lighter than the Fw 190A-8.

The climb rate was also greatly improved. The La-7 easily out climbed the Fw 190A-8 at altitudes up to 5000 meters (16,404 feet). The La-7 reached this altitude in 4.95 minutes, while the Fw 190A-8 required six minutes. The La-7 was also more maneuverable than the Focke Wulf at any altitude, taking only 20 seconds for 360 degree turn versus the German fighter's 26 seconds. The only shortcoming was the La-7's reduced range when compared to the La-5FN. The La-7 had a range of 655 km (407 miles) — 120 km (75 miles) less than its predecessor.

The La-7 could carry a single bomb up to 100kg (220 lbs) under each wing. The La-7's primary mission was that of a fighter and bomb racks were rarely used. The supercharger inlet in the wing root leading edge has been covered — a normal procedure when the aircraft was parked. (Ivan Ivanov)

La-5FN

La-7 Strut

La-7

Revised Shape Bulges Eliminated

The cockpit of the La-7 was spartan by western standards. Wartime La-7s lacked an artificial horizon which hindered flying in poor weather and darkness. The post-war Czech Air Force added additional instrumentation to their La-7s. (Harry Wisch)

The La-7 was equipped with the PBP-1B (Prizel dlya Bombometaniya S Pikirovaniya [Bomb Sight for Dive Bombing]) gun sight. The PBP-1B was a rather rudimentary reflector sight with two deflection rings: one for 200 kmh (124 mph) and one for 300 kmh (186 mph). It was unable to provide any fine degree of deflection that often required firing in front of, through, and behind the target to ensure hits. (Harry Wisch)

The La-5 series and La-7s were usually armed with a pair of 20mm ShVAK cannon with 200 rounds per gun stored in removable boxes. On the La-7 spent cartridges were ejected through circular apertures below the fuselage. The small rectangular exhaust stack cover was a standard feature of the La-7. The La-5FN used a larger cover for the clustered exhaust stubs. (Vladimir Danda)

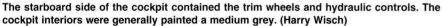

The starboard side of the cockpit contained the trim wheels and hydraulic controls. The cockpit interiors were generally painted a medium grey. (Harry Wisch)

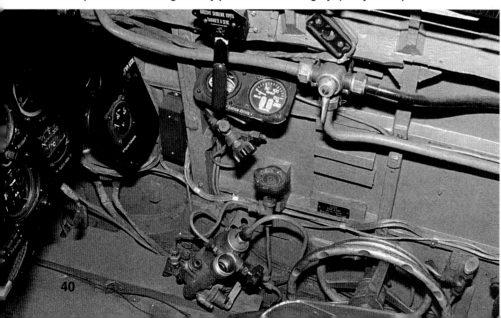

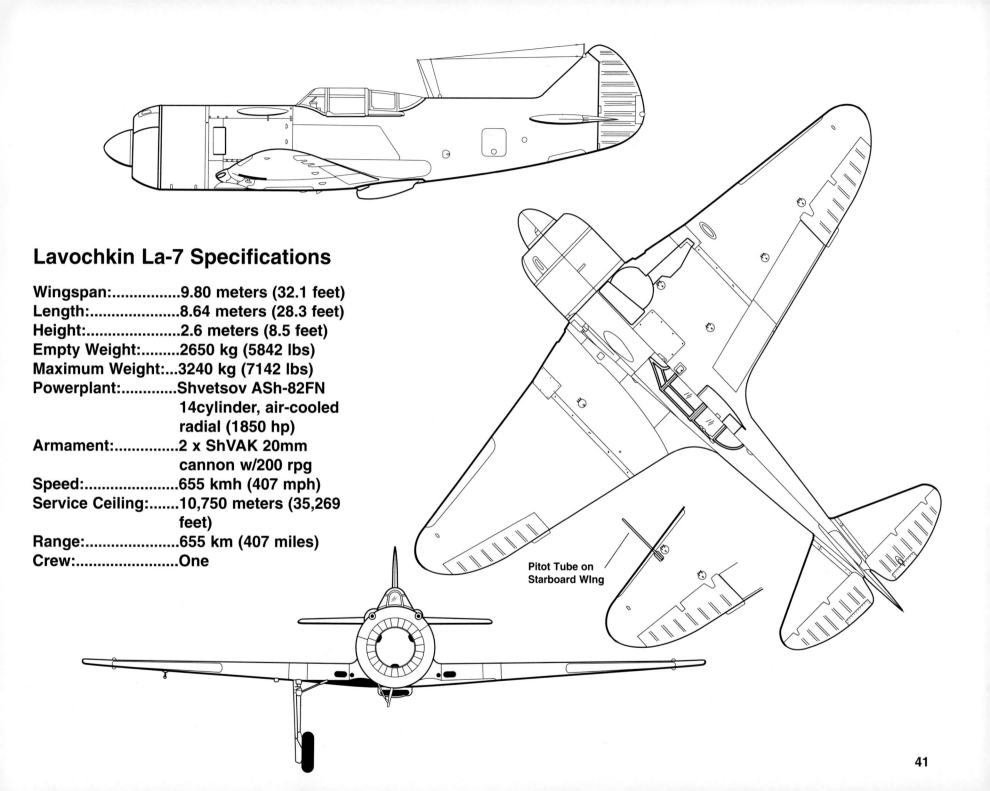

Lavochkin La-7 Specifications

Wingspan:................9.80 meters (32.1 feet)
Length:....................8.64 meters (28.3 feet)
Height:....................2.6 meters (8.5 feet)
Empty Weight:.........2650 kg (5842 lbs)
Maximum Weight:...3240 kg (7142 lbs)
Powerplant:.............Shvetsov ASh-82FN
                        14cylinder, air-cooled
                        radial (1850 hp)
Armament:...............2 x ShVAK 20mm
                        cannon w/200 rpg
Speed:.....................655 kmh (407 mph)
Service Ceiling:.......10,750 meters (35,269
                        feet)
Range:.....................655 km (407 miles)
Crew:.......................One

Pitot Tube on
Starboard Wing

The first La-7 left the production line in May of 1944 and by June the first 57 fighters were delivered to a few regiments for operational testing. By July of 1944 the number of fighters had risen to 108. Through September of 1944 the Soviet Air Force inventory included only 225 La-7s.

The first production La-7s were allocated to the 176th Guards Fighter Aviation Regiment. This was not by accident since Ivan Kozhedub, the top scoring ace of the Soviet Air Force at the time, was flying as a deputy commander in this regiment. Kozhedub ultimately scored 17 of his 62 kills while flying the La-7 including a Messerschmitt Me 262 jet fighter flown by Unteroffizier K. Lange shot down on 15 February 1945.

Between 15 September and 15 October 1944 the 63rd Guards Fighter Aviation Regiment flew the La-7 from Shyaulay and Purachay airfields in Lithuania. During that period a total of 116 group sorties were performed, the majority of them being bomber escort missions and missions providing fighter cover for the fast moving ground forces. Forty-seven encounters with enemy aircraft were reported with 39 of these developing into air engagements. Ninety-four percent of the engagements were against Fw 190s while the remainder were against Messerschmitt Bf 109s (indicating that the Fw 190 was Germany's principal fighter on the Eastern Front by the fall of 1944). During this time, the 63rd Guards Fighter Aviation Regiment scored 55 victories — 52 Focke Wulfs and three Bf 109s — for the loss of only four La-7s.

Among the other units operating the La-7 was the 9th Guards Fighter Aviation Regiment of the 8th Air Army which supported the 4th Ukrainian Front. This elite unit included such aces as Sultan Amet-Khan (30 victories plus 19 shared), Alexey Alelyukhin (40 victories plus 17 shared), Vladimir Lavrinenkov (35 victories plus 11 shared), and Aleksandr Karasev (30 victories plus 11 shared).

During the La-7's front-line service, a number of shortcomings were noted by the pilots who flew it in combat. Many pilots objected to the poor operation of the seat harness which limited their freedom of movement within the cockpit. Another complaint was the lack of an artifi-

La-7 Cannon Configurations

La-7 (2xShVAK Cannon)

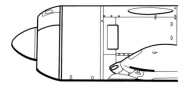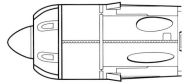

La-7 (3xBerezin B-20 Cannon)

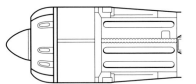

cial horizon which made instrument flying very difficult. Another trend observed during operations was the increase in the number of engine failures while operating from unprepared airfields. It soon became clear that these failures were caused by dust entering the engine air intakes. With the La-5FN, which had its intake on top of the cowling, these engine failures were rare. The problem also did not occur during the State Acceptance Evaluation because the La-7 was test flown from snow covered fields where dry, powdery dust was certainly not a problem. The addition of dust filters alleviated most of the engine failure problems, but other problems, such as those with the seat harness and artificial horizon, were not solved before the end of the war.

La-7s are lined up at the end of the Great Patriotic War. The La-7 in the center carries a non-standard tactical number (believed to be yellow 06) and is equipped with three Berezin 20mm B-20 cannons. The La-7 on the right is an early version with two 20mm ShVAK cannons. (Ivan Ivanov)

La-7 (white 68) is equipped with three 20mm Berezin B-20 cannons which are covered by long symmetrical fairings. The fuselage insignia is smaller than usual. (Nigel A. Eastaway)

Not all La-7s produced were sent to the Fighter Aviation Regiments. During December of 1944, a number of La-7 production batches from the State Aircraft Factory 21 at Nizhny-Novgorod were found to have defective wing structures making them prone to shedding their wings in a dive. The defect was traced to manufacturing faults in the metal spars. Large numbers of the defective La-7s were flown to Lvov (Lemberg) airfield and covered with white sheets where they awaited field modifications to correct the fault.

During 1944 a total of 1782 La-7s were produced of which 1529 aircraft were delivered to the front. Between January and April of 1945 a further 2195 La-7s were built and 1913 of these were sent to the front-line fighter regiments. An additional 1928 La-7s were produced from May to December of 1945. A total of 5905 La-7s left the State Aircraft Factories before production came to a halt in December of 1945. Most of the La-7s were produced at GAZ-21 at Nizhny-Novgorod. A number of these La-7s had a small white Cyrillic inscription 'Workers of Gorky' painted on the port side of the fuselage behind the canopy glazing. Additional La-7s were manufactured at GAZ-99 at Ulan-Ude and GAZ-381 at Yaroslav.

The La-7 was by far the most outstanding radial engined fighter in the Soviet Air Force inventory during WW II. Together with the Yakovlev Yak-3 and Yak-9P, it was superior to the Focke Wulf Fw 190s and the Messerschmitt Bf 109G-10s operating on the Eastern Front. The success of the La-7 was based not only on its design, but was also the result of improved Soviet pilot training during the second half of the Great Patriotic War, while at the same time the skill levels of the Luftwaffe's fighter pilots fell into sharp decline.

Like the La-5 series, the La-7 did not last long in Soviet service since the aircraft had been developed under the assumption that its combat life would be shorter than its airframe life. The airframe was supposed to last three years if kept in hangars. War-time production also omitted anti-fungal treatments of the wood. In the colder northern climes this was not a problem, but aircraft in the warm and humid southern and eastern parts of the USSR suffered greatly. There was one instance of an entire La-7 Regiment being sent to the Far East during the fall of 1945 and having all of its aircraft being struck off charge due to airframe deterioration before flying a single sortie.

After the war the need for such hastily designed and built aircraft diminished rapidly. A shortage of dural and other light alloys were also a thing of the past and all-metal aircraft became the order of the day. The La-7 was soon being replaced by more advanced fighters (including jets) and, by early 1947, the wooden fighters had been completely withdrawn from the inventory of the Soviet Air Force.

Most La-7s were delivered in a camouflage and markings scheme that was virtually identical to the La-5FN. After the war a number of La-7s were delivered with the upper surfaces in an overall grey-green or light grey scheme while the under surfaces remained light blue. La-7s also used the same type of national markings and tactical numbers as the La-5FN although some regiments overpainted the factory tactical numbers on their La-7s and repainted the numbers in a smaller size.

The La-7 logo — a yellow disc with a red Cyrillic 'La-7' — was often painted on both sides of the engine cowling and the tail. The yellow disk was outlined in red. Not all La-7s carried the logo since it was either not applied at the factory or was overpainted in the field. Front-line regiments sometimes applied local recognition markings to the aircraft in the form of white, red, or blue spinners. Yellow was seldom used because it was used as a theater recognition marking by the Germans and their allies flying on the Eastern Front.

Czechoslovak La-7s

Outside the Soviet Union, only Czechoslovakia operated the La-7 fighter. In late March of 1945 the first eight La-7s were delivered to the 2nd Czechoslovak Fighter Regiment at Balice Airfield near Krakow, Poland. During April of 1945 another 46 La-7s were delivered to the 1st and 2nd Czechoslovak Fighter Regiments. These aircraft were too late to see combat since the war in Europe ended on 8 May 1945. Most of the Czech Lavochkins carried the standard Soviet Air Force camouflage and markings, but the La-7s of the 1st Czechoslovak Fighter Regiment had a large red arrow with a white outline painted on the engine cowling. The spinner was painted in white, blue, and red — the national colors of Czechoslovakia.

Czechoslovakia eventually received a total of 56 La-7s. In Czech service the fighters were designated S-97 (S for *Stihacka* [Fighter]). Soviet camouflage and tactical numbers were retained on the aircraft, but the Soviet national markings were replaced by Czech national markings. Later the Czechoslovak La-7s were given a new camouflage scheme of overall brownish-green upper surfaces and pale blue under surfaces. The original Soviet two-digit tactical number was replaced by a four character letter code that was painted in white on the rear fuselage. Occasionally the number was repeated in black on the wing under surfaces.

The majority of the Czech La-7s were equipped with the two 20mm ShVAK cannons, however a few were received with the heavier armament of three 20mm B-20 cannons. These aircraft were also equipped with a direction finding loop behind the radio mast.

Most of the La-7s were allocated to the Czech 4th Air Division which had its bases in the Slovakian (eastern) part of the country. The aircraft were sheltered in order to protect them from the ravages of the climate for as long as possible.

At the same time a Soviet team of specialists was examining the La-5FNs in Czech service during 1946, the newer La-7s were also under scrutiny. Although La-7s in Soviet service were phased out in early 1947, the fighters soldiered on in the Czech Air Force until 1950 making Czechoslovakia the longest operator of the Lavochkin La-7 fighter.

This La-7 (s/n 45 21 08 49/white 49) was among the first batch of La-7s assigned to the Czechoslovak Fighter Regiment at Balice, Poland. The fighter is equipped with a device on top of the front canopy to compensate the compass. The inscription on the fuselage between the national marking and the tactical number reads Workers of Gorky, indicating the aircraft was manufactured at State Aircraft Factory 21. (Ladislav Valousek)

(Below) This Czech Air Force La-7 (white PL-02) is equipped with three 20mm Berezin B-20 cannons. The La-7 is equipped with a radio direction finding loop behind the main radio mast. It also appears to have some of the glazing broken out of the canopy frames. This photograph was taken during August of 1957 at Olomouc-Holice airfield in Slovakia, after the La-7s had been phased out of service. The man standing on the wing is Milan Friso, who subsequently became an inspector of the Slovakian airline Slovair. (Zdenek Titz)

(Above) This La-7 (s/n 45 21 12 33/white 33) crashed at Piestany airfield in Slovakia during 1946. The Lavochkin has a red arrow, outlined in white, painted on the nose and a white-blue-red spinner representing the national colors of Czechoslovakia. The original Soviet Air Force camouflage and tactical number are unchanged, but the Soviet red star has been replaced by the Czech national markings. The La-7 logo was applied on the engine cowling and the tail. (Zdenek Titz)

La-7 Front Fuselage Development

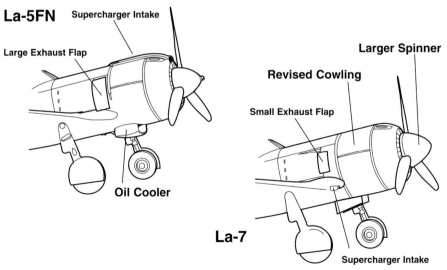

La-7TK

Shortly after the first La-7s left the State Aircraft Factories during May of 1944, a project was initiated to improve the fighter's high altitude performance. The project involved fitting a new supercharger to the Shvetsov radial engine. The experimental Lavochkin fighter received the designation La-7TK.

A production La-7 was equipped with a TK-3 supercharger on each side. The TK-3 supercharger was developed by the Central Aero-Engine Institute (TsIAM). The idea of equipping Soviet fighters with superchargers was not entirely new. During late 1939 a single I-153V (*Vysotnyi* [High Altitude]) biplane had been equipped with a pair of TK-3 superchargers in order to improve the service ceiling and climbing capabilities of the original I-153 design. Instead of the La-7's VISh-105 V-4 propeller, the La-7TK reverted to the VISh-105V propeller of the La-5FN. The La-7TK was also fitted with a starter dog on the spinner.

The outlet cover panel was enlarged and a triangular fairing was added to each side of the engine cowling. The fairing housed the exhaust stub of the TK-3 supercharger. The La-7TK was equipped with two outlet louvers on the square shaped exhaust shield.

The armament of two 20mm ShVAK cannons was deleted from the La-7TK prototype and the cannon ports in the upper cowl were faired over. Additionally, the cannon breech fairings on the engine accessory bay access panel were also deleted. The La-7TK carried the standard camouflage and national insignia for contemporary La-7 fighters, however, no tactical number was applied to the prototype.

The factory test flights of the La-7TK began in July of 1944 and lasted one month. The two TK-3 superchargers enabled the La-7TK to climb to 11,800 meters (36,089 feet) which was 1000 meters (3280 feet) higher than the ceiling of La-7s. A top speed of 676 kmh (420 mph) was accomplished at an altitude of 8000 meters (26,246 feet). This was 21 kmh (13 mph) greater than the top speed of the production La-7.

Although the test results were favorable, the majority of aerial engagements on the Eastern Front were performed at altitudes between 1000 and 5000 meters (3280 - 16,404 feet). Consequently, the need for a high altitude fighter was of a relatively low priority. Additional testing also revealed that the TK-3 superchargers were unreliable. Nevertheless, during the course of 1944 a batch of ten La-7TK fighters were built. They were intended for operations against German high altitude reconnaissance aircraft and were armed with a single 20mm ShVAK cannon mounted on the port side of the fuselage.

La-7TK Development

La-7

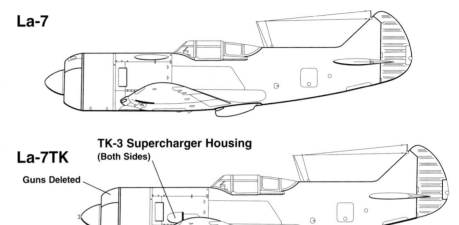

La-7TK

TK-3 Supercharger Housing
(Both Sides)

Guns Deleted

The La-7TK was equipped with a VISh-105V propeller and a starter dog instead of the VISh-105V-4 propeller without a starter dog used on the La-7. The two TK-3 superchargers gave the La-7TK a maximum ceiling of 11,800 meters (38,713 feet). (Ivan Ivanov)

The La-7TK was equipped with a pair of TK-3 superchargers — one on each side of the fuselage. No armament was carried on the prototype. The tail wheel and propeller are missing. (Ivan Ivanov)

Lavochkin La-7R

During the summer of 1944 the first reports of the German Messerschmitt Me 262 jet fighter-bomber and the Arado Ar 234 jet bomber arrived at the Kremlin. The Soviet government fully understood that it had no interceptor in the inventory that could stop the German jets. The Soviet High Command was particularly concerned that jet bombers would be used against the USSR, particularly in raids on Moscow.

As a countermeasure a rocket-powered variant of the La-7 fighter was developed during August of 1944. Top priority was given to the project and an RD-1 rocket motor was provided by a design team headed by Valentin Petrovich Glushko. During July of 1940 Glushko worked at the Reaction Motor Institute in Moscow and had presented a concept of an auxiliary rocket motor attached to piston engined aircraft. The addition of a rocket motor could provide certain tactical benefits such as speeding an intercept, allowing effective pursuit of an escaping enemy aircraft, or allowing the fighter to escape superior enemy aircraft.

The rocket motor's development began in 1941 at the Experimental Design Bureau 16 at Kazan under the control of Glushko. The program received a boost when the leading Soviet rocket motor scientist, Sergej P. Korolyov, joined the staff. By 19 November 1942 Korolyov headed Group 5 of the Experimental Design Bureau 16 and had started work on RD-1 (RD=*Reaktivny Dvigatel* [Reaction Engine]) auxiliary rocket motor. The first trials of the motor mounted on a modified Pe-2RD bomber began on 1 October 1943, although there were some minor setbacks that delayed the program.

By the summer of 1944, production of the La-7 as the USSR's premier fighter was already underway. One example was chosen to test the RD-1KhZ rocket motor. The airframe and wings of an La-7 were heavily modified and the rocket motor attached to the fifteenth bulkhead adjacent to the vertical stabilizer. Its location required the raising of the horizontal tail surfaces as well as enlarging the surface area of both the vertical and horizontal tail surfaces. The rudder trim tab was also enlarged. The fuselage was lengthened by 80mm (3.14 inches) to 8.75 meters (28.7 feet).

The RD-1KhZ rocket engine was powered using a 90 liter (23.7 US gal) tank of kerosene and a 180 liter (47.5 US gal) tank of nitric acid placed in the fuselage. The nitric acid tank was made of stainless steel. The fuel capacity gave the rocket engine a thrust duration of 3.5 minutes. Special pumps driven by the ASh-82FN radial engine supplied the rocket motor with both fuel components.

The addition of the rocket motor and the fuel tanks shifted the center of gravity towards the tail. Consequently, it was necessary to add ballast to the engine mounts to bring the center of gravity to within acceptable limits. The supercharger intake ducting was relocated from the wing roots to the top of the cowl in a manner similar to the La-5FNs. The wing root intakes were faired over. Additionally, insulation was added around the nitric acid tank to isolate it from the ASh-82FN's air induction system. Behind the canopy the radio mast and aerial stub on the vertical stabilizer were deleted. The antenna wire simply ran from the fin to a hole in the rear section of the canopy glazing. The La-7R also had the seat back and head armor removed in a further effort to save weight. (Theoretically, the armor was not needed since the La-7R could speed away from any threat behind it.) The gross weight of the La-7R was 3490 kg (7694 lbs). This was 270 kg (595 lbs) more than the production La-7 fighters. The RD-1 rocket engine and its components alone weighed over 100 kg (220 lbs).

The La-7R carried the standard camouflage of contemporary Lavochkin fighters — dark grey and medium grey-green upper surfaces with light blue under surfaces. The insignias were also

La-7R Development

La-7

La-7R

Relocated Supercharger Intake

Enlarged Tail

RD-1KhZ Rocket Motor

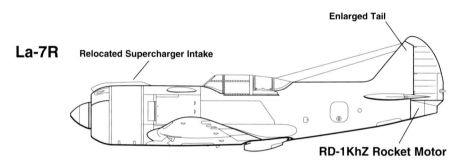

The La-7R was evaluated during early 1945. The La-7R had a similar supercharger intake trunk fairing to the La-5FN. Only two La-7Rs were built. One was destroyed during the testing program. (Ivan Ivanov)

identical to those used on production La-7s. No tactical number was applied to the La-7R.

During late 1944 the La-7R took off for the first time with test pilot G. M. Shiyanov at the controls. The flight was of short duration since a malfunction in the fuel supply occurred once the rocket engine was ignited. The design team was forced to spend additional time redesigning the fuel system. Eventually the fuel supply was placed into a pressure tank and, after some additional minor modifications the RD-1KhZ rocket motor worked flawlessly.

The RD-1KhZ rocket motor provided 3.5 minutes of boost at 300 kg (661 lbs) of thrust. During the flight trials, speeds up to 743 kmh (461 mph) were recorded — 88 kmh (54.6 mph) faster than standard La-7s. When the rocket motor was not operating, however, the system was simply dead weight that adversely effected the performance, in particular the maneuvrability, of the La-7R.

The experience and data gained during the trials of the first La-7R were used in the second experimental aircraft. In contrast to the first La-7R the second aircraft rocket engine was ignited electrically. The second La-7R first flew in March of 1945. During the evaluation the aircraft reached a speed of 795 kmh (494 mph) at 6300 meters (20,669 feet). During one flight the La-7R reached an altitude of 13,000 meters (42,650 feet), nearly 2000 meters (6560 feet) above the service ceiling of a production La-7. Further testing showed that the electric ignition system proved to be troublesome, especially at high altitudes. The electrical ignition system was deleted in favor of a chemical ignition system.

Although the performance of the La-7R was promising, the operation of the RD-1KhZ rocket motor was extremely dangerous. The motor exploded twice during test, once on the ground and once on a test flight. During the test flight, pilot G. M. Shiyanov succeeded in bringing the La-7R safely back to base, but with a considerable part of the aft control surfaces missing. Further testing demonstrated that, although mating a rocket engine onto the La-7 airframe was technically possible, it was unsuitable for service use. The end of the war also hastened the end of the project as did the development of reliable (for the time) jet engines. The surviving La-7R was demonstrated to the public during the Tushino air display at Moscow on 19 August 1946. Its presence marked the end of the evolution of Russian fighters with mixed power sources. It was clear to both the Kremlin and Soviet Air Force that the future belonged to jet aircraft.

The La-7R had an enlarged tail and lacked the fuselage antenna mast and the vertical fin aerial stub. The RD-1KhZ rocket engine was mounted in the tail adjacent to the fifteenth fuselage bulkhead. (Ivan Ivanov)

The RD-1KhZ rocket engine was powered by a 90 liter (23.7 gal) kerosene tank and a 180 liter (47.5 gal) nitric acid tank mounted in the fuselage. The engine had a burn duration of 3.5 minutes. Special pumps driven by the ASh-82FN radial engine supplied the fuel to the rocket motor. (Ivan Ivanov)

Lavochkin La-7UTI

During the fall of 1944, the Lavochkin Design Bureau began development of a two-seat trainer version of the La-7 to replace the La-5UTIs (UTI=*Uchebno Trenirovochny Istrebitel* [Fighter Trainer]). The La-7UTI was not handed over for State Acceptance Trials until August of 1945. The war ended well before any production La-7UTI trainers could be assigned to training and front-line units. As a result, flying students were trained on the La-5UTI. Since the training variant of the La-5FN had nearly identical flight characteristics to the La-7 fighter, transition from the La-5UTI to the La-7 was virtually seamless and did not cause any serious difficulties for the pilots. In hindsight, the need for a genuine La-7 trainer was not regarded as urgent.

The La-7UTI was a straight forward adaptation of the single-seat Lavochkin La-7. A second cockpit for the instructor was inserted into the fuselage aft of the radio bay and was equipped with a duplicate set of flight controls and basic instrumentation. Both cockpits were enclosed by two aft-sliding canopies. The fuselage dimensions of the trainer remained the same as those of the La-7 fighter and the La-7UTI was powered by the same ASh-82FNV engine.

In order to reduce weight, the 55mm (2.1 inch) armor glass screen in front of the pilot was eliminated along with the 66mm (2.5 inch) armor glass behind the pilot's head. The 8.5mm (.33 inch) seat back armor was also removed.

The radio mast was deleted and the aerial wire ran from the aerial stub on the vertical fin directly into the fuselage aft of the instructor's canopy.

The armament consisted of a single 20mm ShVAK cannon fitted into the port side of the nose. The starboard cannon port and breech fairing were deleted. The PBP-1B gun sight was retained in the front cockpit. All bomb dropping equipment was deleted.

In contrast to the La-7 fighter, the La-7UTI had a non retractable tail wheel. As a result, the tail wheel doors were deleted on the trainer. A single landing light was incorporated into the port wing leading edge.

An La-7UTI sits on a field during its State Acceptance Trials. La-7UTI featured a landing light on the port wing — an item not found on the single seat fighters. This aircraft has a yellow vertical fin tip. (Ivan Ivanov)

Top priority was given to La-7 fighter production and it was not until August of 1945 that the La-7UTI began its State Acceptance Trials. The trials were far from being successful. Control was found to be difficult due to the extreme rearward shift of the aircraft's center of gravity caused by the addition of the instructor's cockpit. The handling characteristics were considered to be unacceptable for a training aircraft.

The Lavochkin Design Bureau tried to solve the problems by changing the internal equipment layout. By October of 1945 the modified La-7UTI was again submitted for State Acceptance Trials, however, the La-7UTI's flight characteristics were still poor enough to warrant its rejection as a training aircraft.

A further change in April of 1946 led to the engine oil cooler being relocated from its position under the fuselage even with the wing trailing edge to a new location under the engine cowling. The new position of the oil cooler was similar to that of the La-5FN. This modification shifted the center of gravity towards the front of the aircraft to the point where the flying characteristics of the trainer were much improved. The movement of the oil cooler, however, did cause an increase in drag and a subsequent reduction in speed, but this was deemed acceptable since speed was not a prime requirement for a trainer. Further testing revealed that the oil cooler was poorly mounted onto the airframe and, once the mounting was improved, the aircraft was ready for production during the spring of 1946.

In the meantime the production of the La-7 fighter had been phased out and only a very limited number of La-7UTI trainers were built. The few La-7UTI built were allocated to Training Aviation Regiments and Reserve Aviation Brigades. A few also served in the high speed liaison role. Due to the delay in the La-7UTI's production, the La-5UTI became the most important conversion aircraft for the La-7 pilots until the Lavochkin fighter was phased out in early 1947.

As the aircraft faded into obsolescence, it came into the headlines of the Western press when a Soviet Air Force pilot, flying a factory fresh La-7UTI, defected to Turkey from a base in the Caucasus region. This was the first time Western observers had access to an La-7.

La-7UTI Development

La-7

La-7UTI

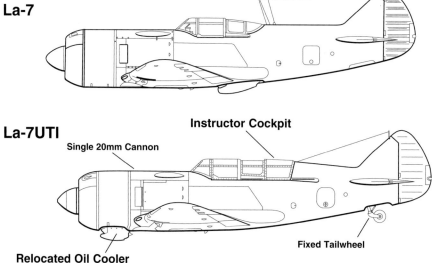

Single 20mm Cannon

Instructor Cockpit

Relocated Oil Cooler

Fixed Tailwheel

(Above) The La-7UTI had an additional instructor cockpit. The aircraft lacked an antenna mast. The tail wheel was locked down and the tail wheel doors were deleted. The Soviet national marking was only applied to the rear fuselage and wing under surfaces. The silver bands on the nose are metal straps used to hold the cowling together. They were often left unpainted. (Ivan Ivanov)

(Below) This La-7UTI, originating in the Caucasus region, was flown to Turkey by a Soviet defector. This was a production variant with the oil cooler placed in the front under the engine cowling. No tactical number was applied to this aircraft. (Heinz J. Nowarra)

Eagles of the Eastern Front

1057 Messerschmitt Bf 109, Pt 2

1073 Ju 87 Stuka

1085 Junkers Ju 88, Pt 1

1142 Focke-Wulf Fw 189

1147 Messerschmitt Me 210/410

1155 Il-2 Stormovik

1157 Polikarpov Fighters, Pt 1

1162 Polikarpov Fighters, Pt 2

1163 LaGG Fighters